JEWS AND JESUS

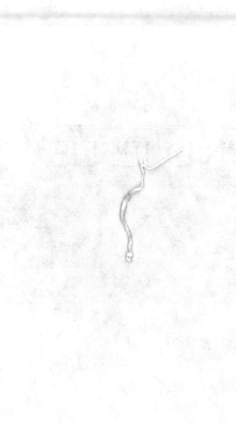

JEWS AND JESUS

BY
ZOLA LEVITT

© 1977, by
ZOLA LEVITT MINISTRIES

Library of Congress Cataloging in Publication Data

Levitt, Zola.
   Jews and Jesus.
     1. Missions to Jews. 2. Levitt, Zola. I. Title.
BV2620.L46   296.3   77-22370
ISBN 0-8024-4335-4

Printed in the United States of America

Contents

1

"To the Jew First"

There was never a greater mission to the Jews than the one announced by the prophet Jeremiah:

> Behold, the days come, saith the Lord, that I will make a new covenant with the house of Israel, and with the house of Judah (Jer 31:31).

This new covenant was not going to be like the old one, which, despite God's good intentions, was consistently violated:

> Not according to the covenant that I made with their fathers in the day that I took them by the hand to bring them out of the land of Egypt; which my covenant they brake, although I was an husband unto them, saith the Lord (v. 32).

No, this new covenant was to have the feature of inner faith rather than just outward observance of the Law. The Law was not to be discontinued but was to be placed within the people:

> But this shall be the covenant that I will make with the house of Israel; After those days, saith the Lord, I will put my law in their inward parts, and write it in their hearts; and will be their God, and they shall be my people (v. 33).

People would no longer have to go about exhorting friends and family to know God, because everyone would know Him:

> And they shall teach no more every man his neighbour, and every man his brother, saying, Know the Lord: for they shall all know me, from the least of them unto the greatest of them, saith the Lord (v. 34*a*).

The people would be able to rest in the magnificent promises of the Age of Grace:

> For I will forgive their iniquity, and I will remember their sin no more (v. 34*b*).

The "fail-safe" new covenant! God would not be remembering men's sins anymore. If men would give heed to this marvelous accommodation to their tendency to sin, their troubles with guilt would be over. They would not, like their common father Adam, have to hide from God in shame. They would not have to fulfill the complex Law given to Moses. They would not have to look anywhere but in their own hearts for God.

And if they stumbled and fell, their Father would forgive them!

Jeremiah makes very clear just who offers this new covenant. The heavenly Father presents His signature:

> Thus saith the Lord, which giveth the sun for a light by day, and the ordinances of the moon and of the stars for a light by night, which divideth the sea when the waves thereof roar; The Lord of hosts is his name (v. 35).

Thus, God signs the covenant. The integrity of the One who gave the sun, moon, and stars, and who administrates the seas, backs this agreement.

And now He dates the contract:

> If those ordinances depart from before me, saith the Lord,

then the seed of Israel also shall cease from being a nation before me for ever (v. 36).

Should this covenant become out-of-date, Israel would no longer be a nation. Unthinkable! God promised Abraham that Israel would be a nation forever, and so it has been to date.

But just so the point isn't missed by the ever doubtful chosen people, God gives the conditions under which He will forsake Israel:

> Thus saith the LORD; If heaven above can be measured, and the foundations of the earth searched out beneath, I will also cast off all the seed of Israel for all that they have done, saith the LORD (v. 37).

Israel is safe. In the day that men know what only God can know—the dimensions of the heavens and how the earth is hung beneath—Israel's security will be in doubt.

When Job sought to question God, the Almighty brought up the same issue: "Where wast thou when I laid the foundations of the earth? . . . Who hath laid the measures thereof, if thou knowest?" (Job 38:4-5).

That settled who God was and who Job was. By the same standard, we see how secure Israel is. And the new covenant is guaranteed by Israel's security. It is as strong as the will of God.

We can see historically how God has stood by His people, Israel. After Jeremiah had told Israel of this covenant, the terrible Nebuchadnezzar of Babylon came, ravaged the Temple of God in Jerusalem, and took the nation of Israel into captivity in Babylon. But God stood by His people, and they returned to rebuild their nation and their Temple.

Then came the mighty Persians, who determined whether millions lived or died. But little Israel remained intact.

Alexander and the Greeks came and went, but Israel remained.

Then came the Romans, the most crushing military force the world had ever seen. They conquered the Holy Land and oppressed the Jews. They threw down the second Temple. Finally, they exiled the Jews from their promised land, and the worldwide dispersion continued almost two thousand years.

But all those mighty conquerors are gone. God had promised His friend Abraham, "I will . . . curse him that curseth thee" (Gen 12:3), and the Babylonians, the Persians, the Greeks, and the Romans are gone. Four so-called invincible civilizations have disappeared, while the Jews have survived to return to their beloved Israel.

We can depend on the new covenant. It is as strong as the chosen people.

The new covenant reached its apex with the coming of the Messiah. God had promised His people a Saviour on earth and had foretold the Saviour's sacrificial mission (Isa 53). The Messiah would bear the sins of men so that the forgiveness of the new covenant would be available to the world.

And so Jesus was sent to His people, the Jews. The Lord Jesus made this very clear. He was the ultimate expression of God's mission to the Jews. "I am not sent but unto the lost sheep of the house of Israel" (Matt 15:24), He told His disciples, and He instructed them, "Go not into the way of the Gentiles. . . . But go rather to the lost sheep of the house of Israel" (Matt 10:5-6).

But, surprisingly, this mission met with only limited success. The Messiah went among God's chosen people, teaching the new covenant and offering forgiveness for their sins. Salvation and entrance into the Kingdom of heaven could be had for the asking.

But the chosen people, rather like their ancestors of the old covenant, seemed skeptical. They asked a great many questions, and they tended to require signs. They were impressed by the teachings and the miracles of Jesus, but their religious leaders found every sort of fault with Him.

The gospels give a picture of a divided reaction. Huge crowds heard the teachings of Jesus and were duly impressed, but we also read of scenes of hushed debate about Him, inappropriate for people confronting their Messiah. We get the impression of only individuals and small groups being saved, but we see a tremendous demonstration of support on "Palm Sunday," when Jews lined the road from Bethany to Jerusalem, crying, "Hosanna [save us!]: Blessed is the King of Israel that cometh in the name of the Lord" (John 12:13).

On that occasion, the ruling Pharisees sounded desperate about the success of Jesus: "Behold, the whole world is gone after him" (John 12:19).

Even foreigners, pilgrims from Greece who came to celebrate Passover at the Temple, requested to see the Lord at that electrifying scene (John 12:20-21).

At His crucifixion, planned by the Pharisees and carried out by the Romans, we see scenes of great lament among the ordinary citizens at the foot of the cross. It is clear that the rulers were not necessarily expressing the opinion of the people at that debacle.

And so the earthly mission of Israel's Messiah ended. Largely rejected by His own people, He was destroyed as a common rabble-rouser by their overlords. But He had left the Jews great legacies. His teachings, the consummation of heavenly wisdom on earth, had been heard, and the stunning events of His ministry had been dutifully recorded by gospel writers inspired by God.

If God would ever have withdrawn His offer of salvation

to the Jews, the crucifixion of His Son would have been the
time. But, as we have seen, the new covenant was immu-
table, and the mission to the Jews continued.

Jesus had promised that the Comforter—the Holy Spirit—
would come to carry on the work of salvation. The Spirit,
who would help Jesus' followers to remember His teachings, would remain in the world until the end of the age.
The arrival of the Holy Spirit was certainly unmistakable:

> And suddenly there came a sound from heaven as of a
> rushing mighty wind, and it filled all the house where they
> were sitting. And there appeared unto them cloven
> tongues like as of fire, and it sat upon each of them. And
> they were all filled with the Holy Ghost, and began to
> speak with other tongues, as the Spirit gave them utter-
> ance (Acts 2:2-4).

A huge number of faithful Jews were gathered at the
Jerusalem Temple to commemorate the harvest feast called
Pentecost (Lev 23:15-22). Many had traveled long dis-
tances, and some had even come from foreign countries,
for attendance was a required rite for the three grand feast
seasons: Passover, Pentecost, and Tabernacles. Jesus never
omitted attending the feasts, despite the hardship of His
traveling to Jerusalem when He was virtually a wanted
man (John 7:1-10). He and His disciples observed Passover on the night before His crucifixion.

So, like Jesus, the faithful out-of-towners had made their
way to the Temple, many bringing appropriate crops
and animals to sacrifice. And they experienced a mighty
miracle.

Acts 2 recounts the incredible scene of Jesus' followers
speaking to the tremendous multitude in all of the people's
own languages. "And they were all amazed and marvelled,
saying one to another, Behold, are not all these which

speak Galileans? And how hear we every man in our own tongue, wherein we were born?" (vv. 7-8).

The foreigners in the crowd were astonished to hear their own languages coming out of the provincial Galileans' mouths. Luke enumerates the polyglot assembly by countries, giving sixteen lands in his list. Far-off Libya, Crete, and even Rome were represented among the gathered worshipers.

There was a confused moment as the strangers tried to evaluate this phenomenon, but Peter rose to the occasion with a wonderful sermon. He taught that what they were witnessing fulfilled the prophecy of Joel, who spoke of the great outpouring of the Spirit upon all flesh. He galvanized his Jewish audience with the tragic story of Jesus, the Messiah. He drew upon the writings of King David, whose Messianic prophecies were fulfilled in the Carpenter of Galilee. He urged them all to seize the moment and be saved.

The crowd was deeply moved, and three thousand people were saved. The feast was a harvest indeed. (At Sinai, three thousand were slain [Exod 32:28]. As 2 Corinthians 3:6 says, "The letter killeth, but the spirit giveth life.")

God's mercy and patience with His chosen people were incisively demonstrated by this miracle at Pentecost. A few weeks before, He had seen His Son executed. He had endured three years of watching the difficult ministry of Jesus and the deteriorated spiritual grasp of Israel.

But, miraculously, He continued the mission to the Jews. Three thousand Jewish people came to Jesus Christ that day, and the Christian Church was greatly amplified. Those who say that the Jews lost their chance to be saved when Jesus was crucified do not see the significance of that great Pentecost day when God, in His infinite mercy, gave His people still another vote of confidence.

Only shortly after Pentecost, five thousand more Jewish people were saved. The Lord had used Peter and John to heal a lame man right at the Temple entrance, and this was seen by a great many people. Peter again held forth, reaping an even greater harvest than at the Pentecost festivities.

This time the rulers became interested and questioned Peter and John with much the same attitude with which they had questioned Jesus Himself. They were doubtful, and they wanted to know to what power the miracle could be attributed. They may have been implying, as they had with the Master, that Satan was responsible for the miracles the believers performed.

The indefatigable Peter saw his chance and witnessed to them. Since the rulers found no good way to quiet them or defame their miracle, the apostles' mission to the Jews continued despite all efforts to the contrary.

At that point there were eight thousand Christians in the world, plus the converts of Jesus' ministry. As far as we know, the vast majority of them were Jewish.

They came into very hard times trying to share the revolutionary faith in Christ (although careful readers of the Old Testament would not have found faith in Christ revolutionary). Stephen, falsely accused of blasphemy, was martyred by stoning, an execution watched approvingly by Saul of Tarsus. Saul, later to become the mighty apostle Paul, at this point was an enthusiastic persecutor of Christians.

The brave mission to the Jews continued as the apostles added to their number and steadily brought their countrymen into the faith.

Then an absolutely startling development occurred. God extended the blessing to the Gentiles.

This was unprecedented in human history, except for the brief mission of Jonah to Nineveh. God had always commanded His chosen people to have nothing whatever to do with the Gentiles. He was emphatic about it. He characterized Himself as "a jealous God," warning His people, "Take heed to thyself that thou be not snared by following them . . . and that thou enquire not after their gods" (Deut 12:30). God had always made a strict distinction between His people and "the other people."

But Peter, visiting the Gentile Cornelius, told his household, "Ye know how that it is an unlawful thing for a man that is a Jew to keep company, or come unto one of another nation; but God hath shewed me that I should not call any man common or unclean" (Acts 10:28). "Of a truth I perceive that God is no respecter of persons," he continued, "but in every nation he that feareth him, and worketh righteousness, is accepted with him" (vv. 34-35).

He then went on to share the Gospel, and "while Peter yet spake these words, the Holy Ghost fell on all them which heard the word" (v. 44).

The Jewish believers in Peter's company were "astonished" to see the Gentiles genuinely converted, the account says; but when they saw them speaking in tongues and praising God, there could be no doubt of the authenticity of their conversion.

When Peter returned to Jerusalem, he had to answer some hard questions about his experience with the Gentiles. The church authorities of Jerusalem—all Jews, of course—were critical of his visiting and eating with the Gentiles, let alone sharing the Word of God with them. But Peter recounted for them a remarkable vision in which God had demonstrated to him that Christ was to be given to the Gentiles as well as to the Jews.

(We may wonder at such a scene. Today it is very often necessary to do things the other way around—to tell the Gentiles that Christ may be given to the Jews.)

When Peter told his Christian brothers in Jerusalem about the unquestionable conversions at Cornelius's household and of the Holy Spirit's presence there, they were convinced. In a decision that changed the world from that day forth, they concluded, "Then hath God also to the Gentiles granted repentance unto life" (Acts 11:18).

After the feared Saul of Tarsus received his Messiah in a dramatic conversion on the road to Damascus, the mission to the Gentiles received its greatest impetus. Saul, now called Paul, was surely the most tireless missionary the world has ever known. Through him, God instructed the Gentiles of the Mediterranean world in his time, and, by means of the epistles he wrote, the population of the entire earth for all time.

But, it must be stressed, God did not discontinue the mission to the Jews. Paul reminds us, "For I am not ashamed of the gospel of Christ: for it is the power of God unto salvation to every one that believeth; *to the Jew first*, and also to the Greek" (Rom 1:16, italics added).

Oddly, almost from the inception of the mission to the Gentiles, men have acted as though God "switched" peoples. This is actually taught today in some sectors. But obviously this would be a violation of the promises made to Abraham as well as the new covenant made with Israel. We have seen that both are in force "forever."

A powerful Christian church rose in Jerusalem, peopled mainly by Jewish believers, as Paul founded additional churches among the Jews and Gentiles of the other nations. The name *Christian* (meaning "Christ in one," not "non-Jew") was applied to the believers at Antioch, and it remains substantially the correct term for *true believers* to the present day.

The mission to the Gentiles prospered so well that Christianity overcame the Roman Empire and, with diverse sects and disciplines, became the most powerful religion in the world. East and West, Christians could be found; and as far as men were able to travel, the faith was shared throughout the known world.

But what about the mission to the Jews? It somehow did not prosper nearly so well. In fact, it would be fair to say that it stopped, despite God's admonitions. Christians, at least Christians in name, actually began to persecute the chosen people.

This showed little appreciation on the part of the Gentiles for the efforts made on their behalf by the Jewish apostles. Probably the bloody work of persecution was carried out primarily by the unbelievers, who followed the cross for personal gain and not "in spirit and in truth."

In any case, the unremitting hatred of the Jews continued in the Church throughout the Middle Ages and into present times.

In the Crusades, the Jews of Israel were murdered, along with the "infidels," by cross-bearing armies from Europe. In the infamous Inquisition, Jews were tortured and executed by the tens of thousands in the name of Christ. In England, under King Edward I, it was enacted into law that Jews had to carry special identification for travel and even wear yellow badges on their coats while in the streets. They were not permitted to leave their homes on Good Friday. A Jew who struck a Christian would have his right hand cut off. Jewish synagogues were suppressed, and rabbis preaching against the Christian religion were burned at the stake. Jewish children were taken from their parents and raised in the Christian religion: the parents paid the expenses. When a Jew did receive Christ, which happened in every generation, his personal property was also "converted" and given to the church. In an incredible perversion of Christian doctrine, bishops of the Church of England forbade Jews even to enter a Christian church.

In France, anti-Semitism was rampant, concluding with the famed Dreyfus trial, in which an army captain was convicted of treason only because he was Jewish. A courageous Gentile author, Emile Zola, rallied to the Dreyfus cause in his book, *J'accuse* (*I Accuse*), which exposed the anti-Jewish corruption in the military. The Jews have "sainted" Zola by naming their sons for him.

The list of persecutions of the Jews goes on without end, constituting the major reason the chosen people will have little to do with Christianity today. Things have not changed in our own century, when Russia and Germany brought genocide to new levels. Hitler remains without peer in the four-thousand-year history of the abuse of God's chosen people.

We must be fair enough to realize that all of these horrors were the works of men. Men kill in any name they choose, even the name of Jesus, that is above all names. The Jew is not accurate in supposing that the Christian religion advocates the persecution of any people.

On the other hand, it's not easy to convince a Jew of that.

❖   ❖   ❖

All that I have written thus far is just to give a picture of what we are going to cover in this book. I am a missionary to the Jews, and having read the foregoing, you know what I mean by that. For our purposes here, it is necessary for all to realize that:

1. God wants the Jews to be saved.

2. Jews are not being saved.
3. The Jews don't want to be saved.

Many fine books attest to points 1 and 2. Any believer who has read the Bible knows God's will for His chosen people, and anyone who has ever been to church knows that it is not coming to pass.

But point 3 has been a mystery for some time. The Jews have never seemed to want their Messiah, from the time He walked on earth to the present day. The bloodthirsty priests of the Inquisition were amazed to see the Jews choose the stake over conversion, and we are still rather amazed today to see their almost endless aversion to Christ.

Few have tried to explain the Jewish attitude rationally. They have just written off the chosen people. After all, they say, God Himself called them stiff-necked, so why bother?

But the Jews have a host of reasons for resisting Christianity or supposing that they do not need it. In this book we're going to review some of the contemporary ones, at least as I see them.

I've been a Jew all my life and a Christian for about six years. I like to think I can see both sides of this question, but of course it is a big question. This book is not meant to be an exhaustive treatment of the subject but, rather, one man's experience with it.

Let me begin by opening my mail for you. As an author of the Hebrew Christian viewpoint and a missionary to the Jews, I get a lot of letters. Some of them are really hair-raising, as you'll see.

2

"Dear Zola: God Must Hate You!"

"The Nazis would have loved your characterizations of the Jews. Too bad they're not still around to appreciate you!"

"Traitor! First you throw away a diamond—your Jewish faith. Then you come back at the rest of your people, defaming them and encouraging them to defect to Christianity. You're the worst of all possible Jews and the saddest of men. You must be very sick inside!"

"You're not a Jew anymore, and you're not a real Christian, either. God must detest you!"

Those statements, paraphrased from letters I received, reflect some of the "fan" mail I get in my ministry as a writer of Hebrew Christian books. I get piles of mail, some warm and congratulatory from Christian readers, both Gentile and Jewish, and some vicious and downright threatening from disgusted Jews, and occasionally from disgusted Christians.

My position is not exactly enviable. My people have historically been hounded to the ends of the earth; few people really love Jews. And my Saviour warned me that I would be hated for His sake; the world has never been wild about Christians, either.

So, as a Jewish Christian, I have inherited, in some ways, the worst of two worlds. But, as "the meek shall inherit the earth," I look forward to better times ahead.

I can certainly understand the attitude of the Jewish people who regard me as some sort of turncoat. There was a time when I myself would have thought that of any Jew who "converted" to Christianity. I was brought up to understand that Christians were simply Gentiles who had styled themselves a religion, however invalid, and that they were very different from the chosen people. For one of us to go over to their camp was not only an absurdity but a serious fracture in the Jewish community, which maintained solidarity at all costs. Many Jews, my family included, made no distinction at all between "Christian" and "Gentile," so that the most heinous persecutors of the Jews were regarded as Christians. (Of course, this was fair to some degree. Many of the most heinous persecutors of the Jews called themselves Christians and, in fact, thought that persecution of the Jewish people was a very Christian endeavor indeed. The Russian Orthodox Church in the Czarist times, the Inquisitors, and the Crusaders, to mention three unforgettable groups of anti-Semites, thought of themselves as Christians. This has hindered the Jews in making the distinction between a true Christian and a common killer who, for one purpose or another, brandishes a cross.)

The Jewish people who write to me have had their feelings hurt, and they sound like it. They are offended enough when they learn of a Jew who follows Christ; it's double jeopardy when that Jew insists on writing books about the matter and going public with it. Many of my Jewish brethren write just to tell me to shut up. Others study my books for errors in either my discussions of Judaism or my estimations of Christianity. A precious few very definitely wish to share what I have and tentatively approach me to find out how I got this way.

I get an occasional letter from a Christian anti-Semite,

too. I do not know any Christians today who advocate the persecution of Jews, but I hear from a few now and then who just do not like the idea of a Hebrew Christian. Almost invariably these are people whose Christianity is based on the teaching of some peculiar sect rather than on the Scriptures, and I often have reason to suspect that they are not born-again believers at all. Some, though, reflect a reasonable Bible knowledge but think that the Jews lost their chance to come to the Messiah at the time of the cross; thus, they think my faith is not valid. Some American seminaries are teaching this crude doctrine today.

Not all of the letters I receive take some strong position. I hear from Jews who are only mildly concerned about my own belief in Christ, but deeply curious about Christianity in general and unwilling to discuss it with a Gentile. I answer questions constantly:

1. Why don't Christians keep the feasts if they believe in the Old Testament, as they say?
2. Why don't the Christians in my neighborhod admit Jews to their country club?
3. Why don't you tell your new friends to support Israel?

My answers:

1. The feasts (Lev 23) were part of the old covenant, now fulfilled in Christ.
2. Some Christians consider themselves an elite group, and they avoid mixing with any minorities—just another sin of sinful men.
3. I tell them every day, but most of them do not have to be told. Bible believers can certainly see the importance of a Jewish Israel to God's plan.

I have an odd ministry of service to behind-the-scenes, religion-minded people. There are lots of people around who wouldn't be caught dead being either overtly Jewish or Christian (and I fear they will be caught dead being *un-*Christian), who still have an interest in God. They are sort of "closet believers" whose meager faith has little knowledge behind it, but they realize that God must exist and that He must have at least a preference in just how He is worshiped. These people can readily believe in the Messiah when shown a few facts from the Scriptures, but they are reticent to come right out and inquire publicly about such matters. They don't even actually *disbelieve*; they merely haven't the knowledge to take one position or the other. They figure that a Hebrew Christian must have a very broad knowledge and an especially understanding viewpoint; since I have been up and down the street, they think I will be ready for anything.

In fact, they stump me all the time; and obviously, if there were no Scriptures available, none of us would know a thing about God. I just try to expose the appropriate portion of the Word to such seekers, whether Jew or Gentile.

I want to share some passages from my letters, concealing names, dates, and details, to indicate the tremendous spiritual energy, both positive and negative, that is alive in the Jewish world. I think these portions of letters, written at great pains and sent to publishing companies with no guarantee of an answer (or that the author will ever actually receive them at all), show that the Jew has many feelings about Christianity. I am afraid they also show, in a rather dynamic way, that many Jews do not want their Messiah.

❂ ❂ ❉

Dear Mr. Levitt:

On one point your book was convincing. Though at first I thought you were a fraud, by the end I was convinced that you are a Jew, albeit a heretical one. As I am any-

thing but orthodox myself, it ill behooves me to criticize
you for that.

Right there is exposed a tragedy of modern Judaism:
this sincere writer is so "anything but orthodox" himself
that he loses a chance to rebuke a so-called mistaken
brother. Many Jews feel very embarrassed about their own
lack of anything similar to faith in God when it comes to
objecting to what they think of as heresy. Christianity,
they assert, is no good; but they themselves, as this honest
correspondent admits, are in no position to criticize. Had he
something like a valid faith of his own—something to offer
by way of contrast—he could show me where I had gone
astray. But consider: he has a conflict of real proportions
in objecting to what I believe, and yet having little with
which to combat me.

I have found that the modern Jewish religion, various as
its forms are, has become so diluted from what the Old
Testament teaches that biblical principles are no longer
understood even by the rabbis. I testify in a later chapter
of my sad debate with a rabbi on biblical matters. How my
heart went out to him for his lack of knowledge of his own
Tenach (the Old Testament). The writer of the above
letter had no real knowledge of biblical Judaism from
which to argue the validity of his own beliefs.

He continued,

> Many Christians (and perhaps you also) will state, "I say
> that Christ is the Messiah, and I cannot be wrong when I
> say that." This is the same as saying that you are infallible,
> that you are incapable of error, at least on this point. But
> infallibility, in most religions, is reserved for Deity. How
> do you end up claiming it for yourselves?

I explained in my return letter that Christians *are* infallible, so long as they correctly quote the Scripture, since

the Scripture is the Word of God. God is certainly infallible, and so is what He said. Admittedly, Christians mis-
understand and misquote the Scriptures, I pointed out,
and then they are not infallible. I asked why he did not
simply consult the Scriptures himself for information about
the Deity and what is reserved or not reserved for Him.

A great many Jews, the vast majority I would say, do
not appreciate that the Bible is purely God's Word. It is
regarded instead as allegory, poetry, a fine expression of
ancient moral standards, and so forth. The Bible needs
interpretation, say even the most learned Jews; therefore,
the Talmud and other commentaries written by sages and
rabbis of past times are given equal weight, or even more
weight, than the Bible.

But I had no better answer than to refer to the Bible.
The Bible makes quite clear just who the Jewish Messiah
is.

The writer went on: "Actually, if Christians would con-
fine their presumption of infallibility to the nature of Deity,
their *chutzpah* [Yiddish: nerve, audacity, or impertinence]
would be less staggering." (This correspondent, comfort-
able in Yiddish, would not have wanted to ask a Gentile
Christian his questions.)

"But as it is," the writer continued, "they extend it to
politics, science, sociology, psychology, etc., all with absolute assurance that they cannot be wrong."

I answered this by pointing out that the Bible speaks to
politics, science, sociology, psychology, and other topics,
and that, again, if Christians quote it accurately, their information can be given with absolute assurance that they
cannot be wrong. The Bible is sometimes brief, but always
unerring, on such matters. And, indeed, believers (and
unbelievers) can rely on what God has said pertaining to
these areas. Our God is well aware of the puzzlements of

human existence, and we have not invented a discipline with which He is not familiar.

"Jesus was neither the first, nor the latest, Jew to be called Messiah," my correspondent went on to say, and, inevitably, "Christians, both the complacent type and the evangelical type, are, in my experience, pretty much the same as non-Christians, with the same faults and same human failings."

I was personally fascinated with the characterization of part of the Church as "complacent type" Christians, and the division of Christianity into "complacent type" and "evangelical type." There is an inherent compliment here for us evangelical types—at least we are not complacent about our Lord; we make noise in the world. But it is interesting to see divided Christianity through the eyes of a Jew. Obviously he prefers the complacent folk, since they never claim anything like "infallibility," but both of his types are just two bunches of ordinary sinners, as far as he can see.

I conceded that Christians of all stripes are sinners, like non-Christians of all stripes, but that Christians are forgiven and are always making the effort against sin, if they are reading their Bibles accurately. I said I thought Christians were "travelers" and had not arrived at a place called "sinlessness" just because they followed the Messiah.

And as to the many messiahs that have come and gone, I said again that the Bible spoke definitively to this point.

In his criticism of Christians for lack of humility, the writer said, "An ancient Rabbi commented about knowing a tree by the fruit it bears." That was intriguing. One Rabbi who uttered that truth was of course, Jesus (Matt 12:33), who was accorded the title *Rabbi* (teacher) by Nicodemus (John 3:2) as well as (unknowingly) by my correspondent.

The writer wrapped up his letter: "I certainly do not want to quarrel with God. But I do get annoyed with those mortals who claim to have a direct telephone connection with God."

Perhaps the Church is doing its job if this man is annoyed by our claim to Christ. Paul annoyed people, and many who confronted the Master Himself were most annoyed with Him. If we are to be persecuted for His sake, we will surely annoy some people. In any case, that seems better than being called "complacent."

Above the signature on that thought-provoking letter was the time-honored expression, *l 'chaim* (Hebrew: To life!).

Please understand that I do not present these dialogues to give an example of how to witness to Jews. I will deal with that later. I only want to demonstrate that the discussion of Christ and Christians among some Jews is most spirited. If we're to testify to this chosen people at all, we should know this. As to my own replies, they are personal choices and, judging by the rather discouraging results (most correspondents just drop me), not the most effective apologetics.

✿   ✿   ✿

A very tough-minded Jewish correspondent wrote one day,

> I cannot comment objectively on your book because I am sure that I will never believe in its purpose [to witness for Christ]. . . . I would find it much easier if you could have written some great pornography—I'm serious, the latter would doubtless "turn me on" a lot more. But your basic premise is what I just can't stand. Sure our Scriptures predicted the coming of the Messiah, but from my view, you could just as well choose Henry Kissinger, for example, and build legends around him!

To get a Jew to admit that the Scriptures predict the coming of the Messiah is not the easiest step to accomplish. Some "spiritualize" the Messianic prophecies in order to avoid having to choose a name, past or future, and to make the Messiah a "concept" rather than a person. We could certainly not "just as well" choose Mr. Kissinger or any other man to be the Messiah, guided as we are by more than three hundred Old Testament prophecies fixing such essentials as His birthplace (Mic 5:2), the time of His coming (Dan 9:25), the nature of His mission (Isa 53), and so many other details satisfied by Jesus. The position that the Old Testament does indeed predict the Messiah, but that He has not as yet come, runs into myriad problems with the Scriptures.

The same writer continued, in the vein of making the Messiah a concept rather than a person, "We [Jews] shall continue to wait for *a Messianic age* and in small ways I'm trying to help to bring it about by direct and indirect actions" (italics added). Between paragraphs, this scriptural analyst switches from a Messianic *person* to a Messianic *age* without realizing the inconsistency. Perhaps it would have been dangerous to his argument for him to suggest that some future individual is due to come as the Messiah, because that would bring about a discussion of just what the prophecies specify. The idea of the writer's working to bring about a Messianic age is as old as the idea of pleasing God through good works, tried and discarded, with God's blessings, millennia ago.

He goes on, "Maybe the best answer to people like you is [for us Jews] to organize our own proselytizing campaign" (He's too late. Several have been organized, and do I ever hear from them! Reconversion centers—organizations that attempt to "reconvert" Hebrew Christians back to non-Messianic Judaism—have been established in this country and in Israel. The reconversion rate is discouraging, for true believers cannot, of course, be "deprogrammed." The truth is the truth, and it will not go away. Instead, the Hebrew Christians exasperate their would-be "reconverters" with powerful witnessing for the Messiah. The reverse evangelists have chosen a difficult ministry.)

The writer concluded with an assurance that my books are most ineffective in saving the Jews (which I already knew):

> Books like yours won't hurt us much. All of the revenues you earn, including the publisher's take, if divided by the number of souls actually "saved," would probably result in a terribly high price per soul—but, of course, from your view, any price is okay.

I could only wish that this fiery-spirited brother of Saul of Tarsus would contemplate the price paid originally to purchase souls of men by the Messiah whom he has not seen and does not really expect.

Further correspondence with the same writer produced more vehemence toward me, and also some relevant commentary on the positon of the unsaved Jew toward things Christian in general.

> There is some good commentary [in your book], reflecting some research, on the saga of European Jewry ending in the final solution by the Nazis, which tragically erased a substantial part of our culture and heritage along with the victims. [But] as to your attempt to inform your readers about who they are dealing with in the unconverted Jew, it stinks! It seems to be another assault on the Jewish community by an over-zealous, self-appointed "specialist." As an intelligent, well-educated person who has become a believer, you could employ your considerable skill in persuading or soft-selling weak Christian gentiles to become true believers.

The term "weak Christian gentiles" is food for thought. In the mind of the Jew, not a great many Gentiles who claim Christ are convincing examples of "true believers." "Out of the mouths of babes . . ."

My correspondent went on with a word of advice as to how I might better relate to my people:

> Try to adopt a true ecumenical spirit in relations with Jews. Let them remain unsaved, and continue to share social and cultural interests which you have in common. My own creed is still subject to modification and maybe I'm becoming more of an ethical culturist—but your Jesus remains a great teacher and that's all. Pure, undiluted monotheism suits me fine.

That final paragraph shows the most dangerous characteristics of the present Jewish concepts of God, Judaism, and life in this world. The "ecumenical spirit" is, of course, of the Antichrist and will result in the most heinous persecution of the Jews in history; the Nazis did not perpetrate the *final* solution to what they called "the Jewish problem." I wouldn't dream of acting in the ecumenical spirit, which says that I should treat Jews as if their faith, or lack of it, is perfectly acceptable to God. If I did this, I would condemn my people to death—not death of the body, as they fear from so many quarters, but death of the soul, the final death. "Let them remain unsaved," advises my correspondent, hoping to persuade me to desist from what is clearly God's will in both Testaments.

Finally, "My own creed is still subject to modification." Here is the ultimate tragedy of modern Judaism: the people whom God chose, who had His Word two thousand years ahead of the rest of the world, still have only the haziest grasp of what a "creed" really amounts to as far as God is concerned. Jesus is reduced to a great teacher, patronized away with any number of appreciated philos-

ophers, and "undiluted monotheism" is the grand title
given to apostate Judaism.

Like Nicodemus, my partner here is intellectual and a
well-spoken leader among his people, but he has no real
appreciation of the spiritual life. Nicodemus also considered the Lord to be a great teacher, and said as much,
but his mind was open when the Teacher spoke.

❖   ❖   ❖

A challenging correspondence was begun one day when
one of my books bounced back at me through the mail.
Someone had referred a book of mine to a Jewish friend
and had had me autograph it to that person. The Jewish
friend, who did not consider the gift very thoughtful at all,
took the trouble to send it back to me, with an angry admonition under my signature. The admonition stated that
I had "given away a diamond" in "giving up Judaism."

Learning the address of this displeased reader, I sent
him a letter about Judaism and the Old Testament. I told
him that a good Jew follows his Messiah in obedience to
God's commands.

By return mail, I got a very angry lecture:

> You are not qualified to determine who is and who is not
> a good Jew. Belief in every word of the "Old Testament"
> [the quotes reflect that the writer does not consider the
> part of the Bible commonly called the *Old* Testament to
> be that at all; it is the *only* Testament, in his view] is not
> a requisite to being a "good Jew." No one is qualified to
> judge his fellow man's relationship with his religion, and
> it is especially presumptuous of you who have abandoned
> Judaism to set yourself up as a judge of Jews. Not only
> presumptuous but arrogant. I don't consider efforts to
> convert me or any other Jews as a proper way to express
> love. I find it repugnant.

Enclosed with his letter was a copy of a letter a local

rabbi had written to a Christian magazine editor. The rabbi took vehement exception to attempts to evangelize the Jews, and he was eloquent. His letter stated,

> For 1900 years the church defined her religion to the Jews in one word: "mission." In the past ten years we saw a beginning of a change in that relationship, a transition from "mission" to "dialogue"; however, you seem to want this relationship to regress back to primitive "mission."

This extraordinary rendition of the Church's perseverance in witnessing to Jews is exactly backward. One could only *wish* that the Church had done nineteen hundred years of witnessing to the Jews, with a true sense of mission. Actually, the present times have seen a great upsurge in Jewish mission work and heartening numbers of salvations among the chosen people. The past ten years have been the best of all in this regard, with numerous societies of Hebrew Christians coming into public notice, and a splendid dedication on the part of the churches to return the Gospel to the Jews in answer to God's age-old wish for His people.

When he cites the past ten years, the rabbi may be referring to the ecumenical churches. They witness to nobody, let alone the Jews, and they characterize their relationships with virtually everybody as "dialogues."

Would that we could return to those days of "primitive" missions of the first century, when the mighty church of Jerusalem sent apostles far and wide, and the Jews Peter and Paul changed the world! (It would be interesting to have the rabbi's comments on the fact that those primitive missionaries *were* Jews, after all. The Jewish Christians, famed evangelists and simple neighborhood believers alike, proved to be powerful witnesses for the Messiah.)

The rabbi goes on to say, in his letter, that there will be

no more Jews if they receive their Messiah. They will change into something else. He says, "We are Jews as we are men. The alternative to our existence as Jews is spiritual suicide, disappearance." He continues, "Is it really the will of God who calleth you [Christians] to serve your people that there be no more Judaism in the world?"

The rabbi continues with a peculiarly Jewish assessment of God's plans for the redemption of men:

> None of us pretend to be God's accountant, and His decision for history and redemption remains a mystery before which we must all stand in awe. It is arrogant to maintain that the Jews' refusal to accept Jesus as the Messiah is due to their stubbornness or blindness as it would be presumptuous for the Jews not to acknowledge the glory and holiness in the lives of countless Christians. "The Lord is near to all who call upon Him in truth" (Psalm 145:18).

It is important to realize that this rabbi is certainly not just being shifty and clever with his opposition to missions. He believes, with a fervent, spiritual belief, that the receiving of Christ is anathema and certain death for Jews. He believes that Christians are actually ungodly to disturb the present Jewish faith in any way at all. He actually does think that God's plan for redemption is "a mystery" unknown to any man.

That the rabbi does not grasp the message of the Bible is easy enough to say, but the problem of what amounts to a spiritual insult, as he characterizes it, is a knotty one. True Christians must witness, and a failure to witness to the Jews is a failure to perceive God's will. Yet the Jews consider it altogether arrogant behavior for a Christian to confront a Jew with the Messiah. It is very hard to bring to salvation a man whose feelings you have hurt in such a deep way.

Back to my correspondent. I took him up on his statement that "belief in every word of the 'Old Testament' is not requisite to being a 'good Jew.'" I asked him which words we may no longer believe in. I also asked when we started to disbelieve our Scriptures.

I received no answer on that, and the correspondence was dropped. I do value the rabbi's letter, and I keep it close at hand. It serves to remind me of how sincere, how dedicated, and how terribly mistaken the most scholarly of men can be, outside of God.

❋   ❋   ❋

Now and then I get a letter from Israel, where faithful American Christian tourists take my books to give them out and some bookstores stock them. The best letter was from a Jewish Christian who had many objections to my ministry—objections of an entirely different kind than those given by the many unsaved Jews I hear from. Apparently this good brother thinks that I have become "Gentilized" and that I should be keeping all of the old Law as well as worshiping the Messiah!

He was a most fascinating man, aged and devout, with a long love affair with Jesus already behind him. And he had the very best of American Bible training included in his long life of service: "I have been a *hassid* [Hebrew: saint] of the Lord *Yeshua* [Hebrew: Jesus] a little more than 50 years. I have even attended the Moody Bible Institute and graduated."

But he had a bone to pick with me: "I do not know when you 'believed' in the 'Lord Jesus Christ' but your 'belief' in Him is of the *goyish* [Yiddish: Gentile-type] brand, away from *Torah* [the Law] and *'Idishkeit'* [Yiddish, or Jewish, culture]."

"Take my advice," he went on. "Come live here in Israel for awhile. Here you will lose the *goyish* coloring of your faith. . . . America, with all the good that's in it, is still

alien soil. No Jew can sing the Song of the Lord on alien
soil (Psalm 137:4)."

He remonstrated with me about eating ham, intermar-
riage with Gentile Christians, and other points of the Law.
I wrote back, telling him that I did not ever feel a bit like
a Gentile and that there was "neither Jew nor Greek in
Christ," as I understood the Scriptures. He did not reply.

✿ ✿ ✿

One of the most lengthy and difficult correspondences I
ever undertook was with a young Gentile lady who had
embraced Judaism. She had not gone through any actual
conversion ceremony but simply loved Judaism, particularly its various rituals and holidays. (There is no valid
scriptural procedure for converting to what Judaism has
become; today Gentiles wishing to convert to true Judaism
need only receive Christ. They then become the spiritual
seed of Abraham, as Paul explained, and inherit the new
covenant, the Kingdom, and the Messiah's other promises
to His people. Some synagogues practice a conversion
procedure for Gentiles [not unlike the Catholic "Instruction"], based on teaching them the customs of modern
Judaism. But this procedure fails to take them to a personal God, the Messiah, or the new covenant. Nevertheless,
the ceremony is normally so inspirational and the Jewish
rituals so impressive that the "convert" feels spiritually
nourished and carries on in apostasy with a zeal for God to
be envied by carnal Christians.)

My correspondent was expert in modern Jewish worship
practices and very well read in the commentaries. She
deeply resented what she considered to be a caricature of
the Jews by me in my books:

> Your distortions and misrepresentations of Jews and
> Judaism would, I believe, be very pleasing to Nazis. . . .

> I don't mean to be hostile; I don't think your antisemitism
> is deliberate or malicious. More likely it comes from
> abysmal ignorance of the group you claim to be a part of.
> The pity of it is that your intentions may be absolutely
> great, yet you cater to so many prejudices I hate to think
> of the effect of an uninformed reader. You may love "the
> Jew," but you're being very destructive of any chances for
> understanding. . . . Your "chopped liver" definition of
> Judaism comes close to completely losing sight of over
> two thousand years of religious tradition.

Her final statement might reflect an unconscious yearn-
ing for the true Messiah of the Jewish people who did appear two thousand years ago: I reminded her that the
Jewish tradition is *four* thousand years old. My own abys-
mal ignorance involves the ritual customs of modern Judaism, and I always admit to it. I found it to vary from village
to village in my youth and became discouraged with it
early in my life. I am not conversant with the order of
service in the synagogues or the various new constructions
of the ancient feasts, both of which are pointless issues in
the light of the new covenant. I do not understand the
up-to-date philosophies about the coming Jewish Messiah,
which also vary, but I know what "liberals" are in any
faith, and I do understand the twistings and turnings of
those who have lost contact with God. There is little variation that I can see between the Reform Jewish temple and
the liberal Protestant church. They talk about many of the
same things (social issues, etc.), varying only in their
group orientation to the world. The Orthodox synagogue
is rather like the Roman Catholic church in its dedication
to certain rituals and canon law, and the Conservative
synagogue tries to bring together the more extreme fac-
tions, like the new ecumenical church is supposed to do.
Those outside of God's will, unknowledgeable of His

Word, have a characteristic style that does not really vary, even across the borders of the great religious divisions.

My correspondent condemned herself as unlearned in the Scriptures with the bold accusation, "Only from utter ignorance could you have stated that the Jewish calendar starts with Passover, or that Rosh Hashanah—'Head of the year' or New Year's Day—is the 'Feast of Trumpets'. . . . I don't think you use the word 'Torah' even once."

I was appalled by this. Exodus 12:2 gives Passover as the start of the year, and Leviticus 23:24 specifies the "memorial . . . blowing of trumpets" on the first day of the *seventh* month (now called New Year's Day—her translation above is correct). She didn't even realize that what she has accepted is totally inaccurate according to the Torah. She felt very confident that what she had been taught is actual Jewish Law, where it is obviously, checking in the Torah itself, mere traditions of men. She is an example of how the mistaken traditions go on and on.

This exposes the sad fact that even some of the teachers of modern Judaism are not aware of what the Torah plainly states. What she had been taught is dead wrong and not in the Torah at all. (I do not always use the term *Torah* in my writing, since most of my readers are more used to *Pentateuch*, or simply the names of the first five books of the Bible as they are quoted. I do not think my respect for the Torah is in question here; I was able to tell her that she should not misquote it to someone who reads it every day. Her own respect of it was more in question.)

In the affairs of men, there are reasons the Jews adopted a fall New Year's Day, and I am aware of them. But they are *not* God's will, *not* supported by His Word, and that's all there is to that. I get plenty of Jews coming to me and saying, "But don't you know how this came about? Don't you know our wonderful history?" I do know some of our

Jewish history, and I think it *is* wonderful, but as a Jew,
I must listen to God first and men second, however learned
the men.

In her next letter, she stated clearly and beautifully just
how chosen people lose their way:

> Agreed, I don't know why it's *Rosh Hashanah* if it's the
> seventh month. I'll have to look it up or ask someone.
> [I replied to this that she had already asked me and
> looked it up in the Torah.] Among other reasons, "It's
> Tradition." And here's where you're missing something
> very important: *Judaism is not based on Scriptures alone.*
> Jews were Jews in the land of Egypt long before the
> Torah was given. Besides the Torah there was the *Tal-
> mud*—oral tradition regarding the Scriptures—commen-
> taries by numerous rabbis, an order of service, modern
> interpretations, the *Schulchan Aruch.* . . . Many beliefs
> and customs have double meanings or triple meanings,
> linked with superstition and numerous cultures in which
> Jews have lived. All of these added ideas and practices
> add depth and color and meaning to the basic Jewish
> law. . . . What's the point here? That I can't—nobody can—
> "go to the Bible" and find "G-d's moral judgments and His
> will very clearly."

I couldn't have said it better, or more tragically, myself.
There is the essence of the apostasy of the chosen people.
They have somehow become convinced that they cannot
understand their own Bible and that God's will is a matter
of various interpretations. (She writes "G-d" in a show of
obeying the commandment about not using God's name in
vain. When she writes *God* without the *o*, she is not using
God's real name, the law says. In my own synagogue,
which I attended regularly in my youth, we could pronounce *Adonai* [God's actual name, or the title, "Lord"]
when we had our heads covered, but we said *Adoshem*

[literally, "the name of the Lord"] when our heads were *un*covered. It was admissible to place one's hand on one's head when one wished to say *Adonai*. Such intricacies of the law became second nature to us Hebrew school students, and my hand would automatically shoot up to my head when I would be doing my studies at home with no *yarmulke* [skull cap]. My arm still twitches today when I come to read *Adonai* while reading in Hebrew!)

My correspondent wrapped up her arguments against the Scriptures with this flat statement: "I contend that sages, rabbis, commentaries and a myriad of secular sources are equally good for inspiring modes of behavior; in fact, the Bible would be useless without them."

She returned to this point in her next letter, mainly because I continued to repeat that the Scriptures, and they alone, were authoritative. Her opinion, and mine, of things spiritual were of no consequence when the Word is available, I wrote. I noted that she switched back and forth, occasionally using a Scripture to defend a point, and then later using a commentary or the thinking of some sage, to back up a different, usually unscriptural, point. She defended this: "That's my perogative as a Jew—to *choose* which authority I'll go by among men. If G-d didn't want 'such divisiveness among His children' [author's phrase] why did He give us the power to think?"

She also said, "As you come across to me, you are concerned with changing Judaism and Jews, making Jews into Christians, taking traditions out of Judaism, promoting a faith-in-Scriptures religion that is only a shadow of Judaism as I (and many others) see it." Substantially, she is correct in that estimation of my ministry, though it would be fair to say that I do not regard "making" Jews into Christians as changing them in any way, other than in guaranteeing their salvation and true service of God. I certainly *do* pro-

mote a faith-in-Scriptures religion; I am not aware of any
other valid kind. And finally, as a Jew who does know a
few things about Jews and Judaism, I would say that it is
obvious that modern Judaism, as my correspondent described it, is only a shadow of the scriptural Judaism practiced by our ancient ancestors.

The discussion about the authority of the Scriptures
went on and on as the letters came and went. I introduced
Daniel 9:24-25, with its remarkable prophecy of the coming of the Messiah. The seventy-weeks prophecy (9:24-
27) as a whole gives quite a comprehensive view of world
history and the future, in its discussion of the actions of
both the Messiah and the Antichrist. My correspondent
seemed to retreat to a final line of defense with which I am
very familiar among the Jews of today:

> It should be obvious that I don't regard Scripture as in-
> fallible. I'm *not* convinced that just because it's [the
> seventy-weeks prophecy] printed in a certain form in
> present Bibles that it must be true as you interpret it. The
> *Encyclopaedia Judaica* noted that Daniel was written by
> four different Apocalyptic writers, in combinations of
> Aramaic and Hebrew that are very confusing to translate.
> I *might* be willing to say Jesus was *a* mashiach [messiah],
> or "anointed one"—but hardly the end of the line.

This terribly grudging admission at the conclusion was
as far as I was able to move my correspondent in some
seventy pages of typewritten communications! That last
line of defense—that the very Scriptures themselves may
be spurious—is hard to confront, except by going into ex-
tensive apologetics. But when a Jew falls back to saying
that our Tenach may not be true, it is a sign that the light
has started to come in. A Jew can say that this or that
scholar thinks this or that section of the Bible got in spuri-
ously, but if he has ever seen his grandfather kiss each

facing page when opening the Holy Scriptures, he hates to take that position. He hates to have to even utter that *our* Book, *our* Word of God, *our* special legacy from Mount Sinai and our ancient land may be legendary or even contrived. That is a panic reaction among all but the most atheistic Jews. Accompanying that reaction is an inner feeling of conviction: maybe the Scriptures have something to tell us after all.

Repentance may well come at the very end of a life of denying God, as with the thief on the cross, or at the very end of a spirited argument against God. As long as there is a grain of respect for the Bible, the potential for that repentance is there. And Jews, almost all of them, do have a respect for the Bible.

As of this writing, the correspondence with this tough customer goes on intermittently, as it may well go on until the Lord comes to settle the matter. It may seem long-winded and not worth the effort, but it does represent an average case of witnessing to the Jew.

Something might be said about this peculiar ministry of "evangelism by correspondence" between me and my people. Some of the accusations made against me—that I stereotype the Jews, that I have no real knowledge of their heritage or position, that I wish for the destruction of my people—are not really fair. The Lord knows that if I did not love and respect my people I certainly would not go to this kind of trouble for them.

It is true that I am not a scholar of modern Judaism, but my training and upbringing compare very favorably with the average Jewish person's today. I attended Hebrew school and Sunday school, being bar mitzvah and confirmed, and I have been to Israel four times. I lived in a Jewish community as I was brought up, and I understood both Yiddish and Hebrew.

Mainly, I know my people a lot better than the average follower of Christ knows them, and that may be why they come after me with such hostility. They can laugh off a Gentile Christian criticizing their faith, but I know their "faith" and its failings. I have no fear of meeting a rabbi in debate (I will review my debate with a rabbi later on), and the rabbis around me know it. I am not a biblical scholar per se but easily the equal of the typical rabbi. In most cases the rabbis avoid me, though I know of some who read my books carefully for errors and for knowledge of how to confront the Hebrew Christian, the most "dangerous" missionary to the Jews.

Jewish people reading this book may well be furious at what they consider my treachery. Not only have I gone over to the enemy camp, but I make noise about it. I help the enemy overwhelm my own people! I refuse to condone their system of religion, and I speak out about it, offering the Word of God as my authority!

Well, I can only say that I have good precedent in the Messiah Himself. He refused to go along with the system of the Pharisees, those self-important religionists who had virtually made a mockery of the Word of God. He spoke out about them. They were furious indeed, and finally they rejected Him and urged the Romans to kill Him.

I do not expect to be killed, but I am not accepted by very many unsaved Jews who know my faith (other than a few agnostic or atheistic Jews). God's death penalty in the Old Testament is often expressed in terms that cut right to my heart. I have been ostracized by my own people for trying to bring them back to God, and my curse is that of Leviticus 23:29: "He shall be cut off from among his people."

3

"Tradition!"

Never let it be said, regardless of what my correspondents assert, that Hebrew Christians fail to appreciate Jewish tradition. We know, along with all of the rest of our brethren, saved and unsaved, that we are God's own people—the oldest, wisest, most accomplished people in the world.

From us and from no one else came the Holy Scriptures. From us came the Ten Commandments and the rest of the Law in all their majesty. To our prophet Moses, God explained the mysteries of creation. To our prophets of the *Tenach*, He revealed the whole of His magnificent plan for men, from the Garden of Eden to eternity. To our ancient ancestors, He gave the world's oldest and best public health laws, its finest poetry and philosophy, and its soundest knowledge of the character of God.

We invented capitalism; we invented communism. We taught the world its politics, history, and religion. We speak the most sonorous languages, run the most profitable businesses, and tell the funniest jokes in the world. Our one-half of 1 percent of the world's population has won 20 percent of the Nobel prizes. We have the most skillful doctors, the cleverest lawyers, the finest musicians, the deadliest army, and the most important nation in the world today.

"The Jews are the best people," I wrote in one of my books, and I have not received a quibble about it yet.

Now, some of the above may raise some discussion here and there, I am aware, but let it be understood clearly: Hebrew Christians do not think little of the Jewish heritage and tradition. I personally am deeply grateful to God for making me a Jew. I would have been completely successful in this earthly life without the Messiah; add the mind of Christ, which I have now been given, and I am truly the happiest and most satisfied of men, and not limited to a mere earthly life.

Of course, being a Jew isn't all roses, it goes without saying. My people have also been the most hounded, the most murdered, the most spat-upon people in the world. My people have the honor of being hated in almost every nation, a claim no other group can come close to. My people were enslaved over three thousand years before the blacks were. My people were tortured for their faith many centuries before religious persecution became fashionable. My people do not tend to be chosen as quarterbacks of football teams, chairmen of country clubs, or presidents of the United States.

My people have always had to make it some other way and almost always in some other people's country, but they always have made it. Rabbis need never fear that the Jews will be destroyed; God has promised otherwise, and besides, after all this time who is going to succeed where so many have failed?

As a matter of fact, historically, persecuting the Jews has proved to be very hazardous. Four mighty, world-dominating civilizations relentlessly tracked down and conquered the chosen people in biblical times, and now all four are utterly gone, as we have seen. Babylon, Persia, Greece, and Rome all overwhelmed the land of Israel, but now we dig in the earth to find their artifacts because their one-time omnipotent empires have vanished. Invasion of Israel is punishable by extinction. But the Jew is found in the same place he was when they came.

The likes of Pharaoh, the terrible Nebuchadnezzar, Alexander the Great, Titus of Rome (who was a more efficient killer of Jews than even Hitler), and a hundred lesser anti-Semites are overwhelmed in the end by the patient, indomitable Jews. Dictators die and empires change hands, but the Jew survives it all, keeping Passover, covering his head, worshiping God this way or that, for better or for worse. The Jew will be in his land when the King comes. The Jew will survive in Israel in the very presence of the Messiah for a thousand years in the Kingdom to come, and at length, God will take His exhausted, special children home with Him for eternity.

What on earth (that is, what besides God?) keeps the Jews going?

"I can answer you in one word," says Tevye, the hero of the play *Fiddler on the Roof*: "Tradition!"

The Jewish traditions—some biblical, some ungodly, some picked up from a stream of endless Gentile cultures, some handed down literally from the ancient promised land for thousands of years—make today's Jew a Jew. What holds the Jews together on earth, despite everything, is a set of subtle and beautiful traditions that would be the envy of any worldly society.

Probably no Jew could even number the Jewish traditions. There are many, and they are second nature to the Jews. "There is a way we do things," my father would tell me, and it was up to me to apprehend it. (I did apprehend it over the years; it meant, "We do things decently, accurately, and with plenty of heart. We keep our feasts, we adore our women, we take the best care of our children.

We keep one eye on the Gentile, because he is hostile and unpredictable. We save our money, and—above all—we keep a bag packed.")

My father lived out his philosophy, and it was up to me to do the same. That, in a word, is how tradition stays traditional.

The Jews are very good at handing things down, praise God, and they handed down the Old Testament Law in oral form for many centuries. Checking their version against the New Testament revelations, they did an excellent job. Comparing just the book of Daniel against the book of Revelation, one immediately sees that the two sets of fantastically intricate and cryptic prophecies of the end times agree precisely. (Such inquiries easily put to rest those theories about spurious Scripture or combinations of authorship of the biblical books.) True, today's legal traditions fail to agree with the Torah in many essentials, as we have seen, but this is a matter of apostasy rather than bad memory. When any earthbound thinkers begin to add to or even supplant the Word of God, there will be havoc. But to give credit where it is due, the Jews, with God, handed the world a perfect Bible.

First among the numberless traditions that make up Judaism as practiced is monotheism. The worship of one, and only one, God, is thoroughly and peculiarly Jewish, and it always has been. The magnificent *Sh'ma*, the most reverenced of Jewish prayers, states plainly, with brevity and force, the central principle of Jewish Law:

> Sh'ma Yisroel, Adonai elohenu, Adonai echad. "Hear, O Israel: The LORD our God is one LORD" (Deut 6:4).

Today people are used to the idea of one God, and even the atheists say "God doesn't exist" rather than "There are no gods." We more or less take for granted that we all

have one Father in heaven, and Jews concede that the
Christian God is the same God they themselves worship.
But back in ancient times, the idea of one God was a
startling and original concept. Undoubtedly God placed
a real emphasis, in the Scriptures, on His singularity in
order to draw a clear distinction between Jewish worship
and the pagan worship found around the Holy Land on
every side. The peoples who contended with the Jews all
had plural gods, whole families of gods whose all-too-
human failings had a debilitating effect on their worshipers
and left the people without a spiritual anchor. The mischief
of the Greek and Roman gods and goddesses is well re-
membered today, and even studied by some scholars who
consider this paganism a worthy expression of human religious practices. (These ancient myths do perhaps lend us
much knowledge of human behavior and psychology, but
they are not to be compared in any way with the scripturally ordered worship of the chosen people.)

Now, if everybody today realizes that there is one God,
or if they are disbelieving toward one God, why is the idea
still so precious to the Jews? Well, that's the tradition.
The idea is *our* idea! God presented this knowledge to *us*,
not *them*. That God is Jewish, He didn't say; but that He is
singular, He said, and He said it to *us!*

How I remember how hard we came down on that last
word of the *Sh'ma: echad* ("one"). It was a special pleas-
ure to emphasize our brilliant revelation, which truly
changed the whole world.

From the extreme respect the Jew gives that special
concept, it is easy to see the first bone the Jew usually picks
with Christianity. Christians worship three gods, some
Jews say. There is God, there is Jesus, and there is the so-
called Holy Spirit. This is anathema to the Jew.

Well, it really would be anathema if Christians truly held

to three gods, but of course the Scriptures, including the
Old Testament, show one God existing in three persons.
God the Father is cited in the first statement of the Bible,
"In the beginning God." God's Spirit moved over the earth
as early as the second verse of Genesis: "And the Spirit
of God moved upon the face of the waters." God's Son
(Psalm 2:12; Isa 9:6) is mentioned as distinct from the
Father, with titles such as Holy One, Prince of Peace, the
Servant, and, most relevant to Jewish hopes, Messiah (Dan
9:25).

The idea is not so strange to our particular creation. All
earthly matter (water for example), takes three forms;
nevertheless, the very term *Trinity* sounds antagonistic to
the Jews. Certain sectors of Judaism hold that the Messiah
will be a man only, without a divine nature, in order to
hold that God is *one*. (Moshe Dayan, David Ben Gurion,
and other Jewish notables, as well as numerous historical
figures, have been held to be the Messiah in their times.
Waiting for a human messiah to prove out is discouraging,
however, and the majority of those who believe in a coming
Messianic age, do not expect a personality—human, divine,
or any combination—at all. The Messiah has become con-
ceptualized, as we saw in the letters above, and for many,
the term merely represents a coming time when the Jews
will be at peace. In a way it is hard to blame the average
Jewish thinker for that. He normally has only the vaguest
knowledge of Messianic Scripture, and the wait for the
Messiah has been very long indeed. The Messiah should
have come long ago, or at least He should have come when
He was badly needed, such as in the Nazi holocaust. Since
He has not come in so long a time of suffering, He is barely
expected to come at all. A sad moment in *Fiddler on the
Roof* occurs when the people of the little village of Ana-
tevka are victimized by a pogrom and must give up their

homes and leave. One of them asks the local rabbi if this wouldn't be a good time for the Messiah to come. "We've waited *so* long, he says. The rabbi does not even answer the hopeful question. "We'll have to wait somewhere else," he says, totally beaten.

As the Messiah is not going to come, or at least since it does not look like He is coming, many Jewish people have begun to look only for peace, assuming the Messiah to be "peace." And it is hard to blame them for that, either; they have not seen a generation of real peace since King Solomon!

A few Jews, mainly the Orthodox, do think of the Messiah in the terms in which He is explained in Scripture, and they expect a God-man someday. They examine Jesus on somewhat more sound grounds, but they reject Him as falling short of their ideal of the Messiah. Again, they fail to appreciate many biblical descriptions of the Messiah as a suffering Servant (e.g., Isa 53) and an Intercessor for His people. But at least they see something like a divine nature.

However, they typically fail to appreciate God in the person of the Holy Spirit. It would be hard to find a Jew anywhere who will concede that third personality to God.

The distinction over the Holy Spirit is hairline. Reverent Jews who are aware of Scripture about the Spirit consider that the one God they know simply makes Himself invisible to visit the earth. This is a reasonable construction of many Scriptures but does not answer to the very different ministries of the three persons of God. It certainly does not explain the simultaneous appearances of the three Persons, such as at Jesus' baptism, where the Spirit descended upon Him, God spoke from Heaven, saying, "This is my beloved Son," and the Carpenter of Galilee stood in full view of the crowd at the same time (Matt 3:16-17). But that, of course, is New Testament Scripture.

It boils down to the fact that the tradition of one God will not bear the intrusion of so revolutionary an idea as three personalities of that God. And that is the end of that; the Jews will not believe in the Trinity.

The reason again is tradition, not an accurate analysis of Scripture. But tradition, the hallmark of this most ancient of peoples, has become more fundamental to their "Jewishness" than the Bible itself.

The feasts, or holy days, of the Jews are probably the next most noticeable tradition of Judaism. They are a thoroughly scriptural way to worship God, but they have become changed over the time since they were ordered in Scripture (Lev 23, in the wilderness) and remarkably, one feast has been utterly forgotten and is omitted today. Not surprisingly, that one has to do very intimately with the Messiah and was beautifully fulfilled by Jesus. Its absence in the Jewish year is a clear indication that the Jews do not want their Messiah.

God gave Moses concise information about the various feasts and even gathered the high points into one brief chapter of Scripture (Lev 23) so that no one would make a mistake in this most complex mode of worship. The planning is beautiful and the observances most meaningful.

Passover begins the Jewish year (Lev 23:5) and Unleavened Bread occurs through the following seven days (v. 6). Firstfruits, the "forgotten" feast, is to occur on the Sunday of the week of Unleavened Bread ("on the morrow after the sabbath," vv. 10-11).

It is interesting to consider just how the Messiah fulfilled these three feasts that open the year. He was crucified on Passover (as the "Lamb of God," John 1:29), buried on Unleavened Bread ("This [bread] is my body," 1 Cor 11:24), and raised on Firstfruits (on the Sunday of the week of Unleavened Bread, now called Easter Sunday).

Obviously, this is much more than coincidence, especially as He went on to fulfill the next feast, Pentecost (Lev 23:15-16) by sending the Holy Spirit to the Jews on that exact day. The Messiah thus performed a beautiful and meaningful observance of the ancient feasts, for the edification of the Jews.

To note the remaining feasts, Trumpets is next, on the first day of the seventh month (Lev 23:24); the Day of Atonement follows (v. 27); and the festival year is concluded with Tabernacles (v. 34). The Lord will fulfill these feasts, prophecy tells us, with the rapture of the Church ("the trumpet shall sound," 1 Cor 15:52), the redemption of Israel ("all Israel shall be saved," Rom 11:26) and the establishment of the Kingdom, wherein the Lord's own tabernacle will stand in Jerusalem (see Ezek 37:25-27; Zech 14:16).

Unfortunately, the fulfillments of the feasts have been lost on the Jews for a long time, but more striking is the fact that the feasts have become so changed by tradition that their true meanings have been distorted beyond recognition. Without a close study of Leviticus 23, the Jew of today can only assume that the feasts are mere remembrances of some vague, past happenings in Jewish history. Six of the feasts are still kept by most Jews, but with emphases not at all indicated by the Torah.

The present Jewish festival year looks much different than the Bible presents it, with some new feasts being added and an important old one dropped. Passover is invariably observed, correct to the details of Exodus 12, and with some added artifacts, but Unleavened Bread per se has been made a part of an eight-day "Passover." Thus, the burial of the Messiah is not recognized by the Jews. Firstfruits is completely omitted, and thus the significance of the resurrection has been subverted. Remarkably, although

Firstfruits is clearly ordered in the Scripture, in the very next verse after Unleavened Bread, it is virtually unknown to today's Jew. Pentecost is still observed, in its harvest meaning, but without the recognition of the coming of the Holy Spirit, of course. Trumpets has become Rosh Hashanah, the "New Year," or head of the months, as we have seen in the letters above, and thus a key symbol of the rapture is dropped. The trumpet *is* blown in the synagogues—a ram's horn called the *shofar* is appropriately used—but merely to call the worship together, not as a symbol of the coming of the King of the Jews. The Day of Atonement is certainly still hallowed; Yom Kippur is the most sacred day of the year to Jews everywhere. But tragically, no atonement can be available for the Jews through mere fasting and prayer in these days of the new covenant. The Messiah has already come, bearing the Jewish redemption for those who would have it, but the emphasis in the modern Jewish tradition is still on beseeching God for one more year on the basis of good works of the past year and the complete atonement for sins. The spirit of the feast has been more or less maintained; in ancient times, the Jews were to be conscious of their shortcomings before God on this fearful day. But without a high priest and an offering for the nation's sins, as specified in the Law for this feast (Lev 16), redemption is truly unthinkable. The High Priest, of course, has already come and made His offering; those not believing Him are not participating in the offering and obviously not gaining redemption, however sincerely they may atone. Tabernacles is still kept, in the memory of the shelters the Jews found provided by God in the wilderness, but without the knowledge of the future fulfillment in the Kingdom to come to Israel, where the Lord will establish His tabernacle.

When I attended the synagogue as a boy, I kept each of
these feasts in the tradition of my people, but I had no idea
of their significance. Often I did not even understand the
traditional significance of a given feast, let alone the biblical significance. The services were largely in Hebrew,
chanted in ritual style from the podium, and beyond my
comprehension (and the comprehension of the majority
of the adults of the congregation). It was regarded as
enough for us to join into the holiday spirit with the rabbis,
and the details of the feasts' significance were mostly left
out. We manufactured our own holiday joy.

This Christmas-like approach to something sacred left
me cold, to say the least. I would fast on Yom Kippur,
having no real idea why. I was aware that most of the congregation had been granted another year in the book of
life, because most of last year's worshipers had returned,
but I wondered about all those who I knew were not fasting. Members of my own family broke the fast with a mis-
chievous conspiratorial air, and they still made it to the
next Yom Kippur. I thought God did not keep very good
books or was a most lenient judge. Never, in all of my
training in the synagogue or my years of Hebrew school
and Sunday school, were the actions of the ancient high
priest of Israel explained to me. Never did I realize that it
was the sacrifice made by the priest that atoned for the
people's sins, not their fasting.

If they did not tell me that, they did not tell me Judaism.
Without that one most vital piece of information, I was
merely living out a ritual, a groundless tradition.

Similarly, the spirit in which we celebrated Passover was
that of gaining our liberty, like the Fourth of July. And
this is fine, except that the Lamb who redeemed us was
barely referred to. The angel of death passed over us
because we marked our doorposts with blood, I learned,

but no one ever explained what special meaning this lamb's blood might have had to our God.

If the Day of Atonement and its lesson of sacrifice equaling redemption are the center of Judaism, then Passover, with its most graphic representation of the same point, is at least as fundamental to the Jewish faith. But the significance of both lay hidden in the rituals, and I simply never understood them until I came to the Christians, people who read the Scriptures.

Now, all of this discussion of the changed feasts is not to say that people get nothing out of traditions. The Jews enjoy their feasts far more than most other religious groups enjoy their feasts, and indeed, many Christians fall into the trap of inventing new feasts and forgetting the old. Pentecost, the very birth of the Church, is barely noted in today's churches, while Easter, named for the Babylonian goddess Ishtar, has somehow replaced God's styling of the original, "Firstfruits" (see also 1 Cor 15:23). People everywhere seem to restyle certain essentials of their faith, dropping some items, adding some others, until they get a new tradition together. They then go on in the tradition with much joy, but with a loss of significance that departed long before, when the original observance was forgotten.

I must say that Passover and the other feasts, however we Jews observed them, were moments or rare happiness in the Jewish community. The Jews still relish these re-manufactured feasts, though there are obvious errors. Most of my correspondents take the feasts of today to be very authentic, considering any objection to their style, even an objection based on solid ground in the Torah, to be blasphemy.

In any case, with no separated Unleavened Bread and no Firstfruits, and with the addition of a host of new feasts, the Jewish tradition has overwhelmed the Scriptures; and the festival year, once a central pillar of the Law, has deteriorated into so many cultural customs irrelevant to the worship of God.

One of the most stunning demonstrations of the power of tradition is illustrated in the laws concerning eating. God long ago gave the Jews the dietary laws, and they are conceded by medical authorities to be good laws, sensible and effective. Doubtless the Jews avoided a lot of trouble with poisons and plagues by resolutely sticking to the inconvenient but absolutely sound advice of the Creator of all living things. God meant for His people to survive, and He went to some trouble to assure that.

Because the Jews did not eat pork, they avoided trichinosis, a fearsome, ancient killer. Because they washed their utensils carefully, they survived plagues that exterminated millions. (They were accused of *causing* the bubonic plague in Europe in the Middle Ages, poisoning the wells and all that, out of envy of the Gentile authorities. Local priests noted that the infernal Jews, with their strange ways of cleanliness and peculiar choices of foods, seemed to skirt the plague's consequences, and they thought the chosen people knew which wells were poisoned, or whatever. The Jews, simply sticking to the Creator's advice, were spared mass death. The principle still holds: death by plague or by the wages of sin is still avoidable upon the advice of the Creator.)

Omitting pork and the flesh of other scavengers is one thing; the separation of milk and meat is a wholly different area, for it is not in the Law and is based solely upon tradition. It demonstrates how tradition overwhelms even common sense, let alone Scripture, in the lives of modern Jews.

The Jews today who wish to eat "kosher," in accordance with the Law, are extremely strict in separating milk and meat and their derivatives. Tradition says that this is an important law from the Torah. Orthodox Jews go to great length to keep their milk and meat apart, having separate sets of dishes and flatware for each category. Since Passover (according to tradition) requires another set of dishes, different from those used the rest of the year, the truly kosher housewife has *four* separate sets of dishes and flatware in her kitchen. This allows her to separate milk and meat on Passover as well as throughout the remainder of the year.

Milk products and meat products are also separated at mealtimes so that, for example, a person may take cream in his coffee following a dairy dish, but not after a hamburger. Some Jewish restaurants serve only dairy meals, and others only meat meals, an implicit guarantee that the kitchens are uncontaminated by a mixture of the two types of food.

Once I stayed overnight in a kosher home, and I neglected the law because at that time I was not used to it. I cut myself a piece of cake made with a milk batter, using a knife from the set used to carve meat. My hostess was shocked, but she did not burden herself with the letter of the law (or, more accurately, tradition), which states that the knife must be buried in the ground with prayers of sorrow, and the kitchen totally sterilized from floor to ceiling!

To understand the background of this tradition, let us look into the Torah to find its origin. God says in Exodus 23:19, "Thou shalt not seethe [boil] a kid in his mother's milk." That is the sole statement on the matter, although the same statement does appear elsewhere in the Torah.

The purpose of the command seems to be that God wished to avoid the appearance of cruelty in the Jewish sacrifices. The Canaanites purposely boiled baby goats in their own mothers' milk, according to some pagan belief, and this sort of animosity toward nature appears nowhere in the Jewish sacrifice laws.

But just realize. from that simple prohibition comes the entire tradition of separation of milk and meat! The steps from the Law to this tradition are typical of what will be done by men striving to please what they regard to be a demanding God. First the sages interpreted that there must have been something about the very composition of milk and meat that makes their mixture in the stomach a bad idea. So they forbade eating foods of those two groups at any one meal. Next they noted that ancient housewives tended to wash their day's dishes all together, and that the remains of food from milk meals mixed with the remains from meat meals. Deeming this illegal, they ordered that there be separate sets of dishes and flatware. The entire career of a given dish or spoon would be in the one area or the other, never in both.

And, finally, today we have come to where there are kosher homes with two dishwashers in the kitchen for washing the two categories of dishes!

Again, the true Law, the Torah, makes no comment on eating milk and meat foods together or on dishes; the prohibition on the separation of foods refers solely to sacrifices made in the Temple. But the tradition has overwhelmed the Scripture, and today a "good" Jew keeps his milk and meat dishes, and all that goes with them, strictly separated.

There is still another step to building a tradition that should not be forgotten: it must be imbued with a certain human pride and charisma. Thus, "We do this because we are Jewish!" becomes almost a battle cry. However unfounded the tradition, once it becomes entrenched it is a vital part of what makes the people what they are.

The Jews, of course, are not the only people in the world

to hold traditions more sacred than Scripture; the Christians, even the born-again believers, do plenty of it, too. The simple ice-cream sundae is a case in point. About a century ago, an American confectioner ran out of carbonated water for making ice-cream sodas. To satisfy his customers, he contrived a concoction consisting of ice cream and sauce but no soda water. Now, soda water was held to be intoxicating by the local churchmen, and our friend had trouble enough serving it. But since his new invention, which caught on very quickly, had none of the "intoxicating" spirits, he felt very religious serving it, and he named it "Ice Cream Sunday" (or ice cream *for* Sunday). This raised a lot of ire in Christian circles because Sunday, the Lord's Day, was no designation to tamper with. The confectioner, however, argued that he had bent over backward already to eliminate the offending carbonated water. A compromise was reached when he offered to misspell *Sunday* as *sundae*. And so the whole world follows it.

In the name of keeping some sort of religious laws, men will plainly do the ridiculous, not so much to appear more religious, but because a certain charisma is gained thereby. We all like to identify with a successful group, and religion of any sort provides for a convenient, wholesome identification. For many, worshiping God according to His Word is not quite fascinating enough. It becomes much more absorbing when we build all sorts of unique traditions into our worship and create a style appropriate to our group alone.

So, if tradition affects every group, why pick on the Jews? Well, the Jews had the Law to begin with. In a way, they should know better. In practice, however, they have been at worshiping the true God twice as long as anyone else, and thus they have twice as many traditions involved in their worship. Should the Lord tarry two thousand more years, we might see some real nonsense come into the Christian Church if men forget their Scriptures.

But our subject here is why the chosen people do not want their own Messiah, and this issue is now clear. The Jewish people do not want Jesus because it is a tradition of theirs not to want Him. In some sectors it becomes a distinct law in itself to avoid the mention of Jesus and to regard His name as a cussword.

When I was a child, I loved to sing the Christmas carols in school. But the tradition at our synagogue was that we never pronounced the words *Jesus* or *Christ*. Thus, I compromised, singing the carols with enthusiasm, but dropping out when the Lord's name appeared. I still feel a slight discomfort, or rather a "buzz" inside, when I say His name. In my ministry this becomes a problem, I can tell you!

When did refusal of the Messiah come to be a real tradition? How did that come about? The answer is very simple. People carrying crosses murdered the Jews, and that is certainly all it takes. Nothing more needs to be said. We can certainly explain that men kill in any name they choose, even the name of the King of the Jews. But people don't make fine distinctions between killers, and who can blame them?

And again, we have seen in recent days "Christians" killing each other in Ireland and "Christians" in a shooting war in Lebanon. If you ask the Irish Catholics or the Lebanese Muslims if their enemies are real Christians, they will say that their enemies use real bullets—who cares to make spiritual judgments at such times? Sure they are Christians if they call themselves Christians. Why not? Nobody is checking their biblical orientation during the street battles.

The Jew has a very good point. Martin Luther cursed the Jews and wanted them deported and their property confiscated. He said this in his senility, but he said it. He is quoted regularly and powerfully by the reconversion centers. The Crusaders came to Israel a thousand years ago, singing hymns and wearing crosses and quoting Scripture. On one occasion they amassed the Jews in a wooden synagogue and burned it to the ground. Throughout Europe in the Reformation age, Jews were not permitted to enter the Christian churches, and they were regarded as inferior human beings, not unlike the way Hitler and Stalin thought of them.

I can truly say that if the subtle anti-Semitism I detect around me in the United States someday bursts into flame, I have a very real fear of some people around me who call themselves Christians.

How did aversion to Jesus become a Jewish tradition? The answer is all too clear.

Christians are certainly more enlightened about Jewish people today than they ever were in the past, and it is doubtful that any Bible-reading people ever persecuted the Jews. It is incomprehensible that those conversant with the Word of God could hate His chosen people. But it stands to reason that there is still much to make up for today. If the Jewish tradition of rejecting Jesus and all He stands for is to be relaxed, Christians have a lot to do. Testimony to Jews must be loving, and truly so, and they must be treated like the chosen people that they really are.

Conceivably the devil is losing a long battle. He never tires of Jewish blood, because if he can defeat the Jews, God's plan will go awry. So much of the future depends on the Jews, Israel, and the fulfilling of the promises involved with them. So the enemy has cleverly used men to keep the chosen people from what they were chosen for. He has seen to it that outright unbelievers would appear in churchly robes and pronounce the name of the Messiah loud and clear in the worst of circumstances. He has seen to it that the Jews would begin to actually hate Jesus, one of their own. But today he is losing ground, as accurate Bible study and witnessing churches move toward the Jews with care and with love. As Israel strives to maintain its foothold in this terrifying world, the true Church remains with her. As the Jews struggle in unbelief, testifying Christians witness.

Tradition is a powerful force that keeps people from changing to something better. It dictates a kind of ungodliness that is hard to move, hard to deal with. But it is within the power of those who have the mind of Christ to deal with it.

God is love, and love conquers all.

4

The Jewish Mystique

There is a certain atmosphere—a certain quality—about the Jewish community that I really miss. Things around the Church are not inferior in any way, but just different. It is simply not the same old *havurah* (fellowship) I grew up with.

Some Jewish evangelists feel that Jews who have found their Messiah are orphans of the Christian Church. The new converts discover that they can't practice Christianity through the Gentile frame of reference.

I don't really support the idea that Christians or Jews always have an inferiority complex when facing their counterparts. To me, the superiority-inferiority conflict goes both ways. I know some Christians who lord it over the Jews, and, frankly, I feel superior to them. They don't know their Lord or His Word very well. But then, there are Christians, usually humble and found in the back rows of the churches, to whom I feel very much inferior. They know their Bible better than I do, and they seem to concentrate on loving their fellowmen without regard for anyone's lineage. Like the Father, they are no respecters of persons.

The New Testament indicates that neither society is particularly superior, and in Christ "there is neither Jew nor Greek" (Gal 3:28) anyway. Outside of the Messiah, people are just a mob of indistinguishable sinners; with Him they become a "Bride" of indistinguishable saints.

But the unsaved Jewish community, that group who do not want their Messiah, is our concern here. If you feel inferior or superior to them, that's your problem, but we must in any case look carefully at that remarkably efficient, warm, human organism called "the Jewish community." Its very self-sufficiency, interdependence, and separatism preclude Jesus, and that is where the Church comes in (hopefully).

Discussing the character of a whole community, like the international Jewish community, is certainly a hopeless task. I can relate only my impressions of my own community—the one I was raised in—and other Jewish communities where I have lived. I *can* say that I have not seen a great deal of variation in the character and style of the people from community to community, despite their varied modes of worship. Jews seem to be Jews, with all those identifying traits that they consider "stereotyping," wherever you find them. American, European, and Israeli Jews seem much the same to me. I have met some Russian Jews, and they also fit the mold.

Jews are stubborn, and Jews are kind. They are generous, and they are murderously competitive. They know and respect each other on sight. They love each other fiercely.

There is a certain comradery between Jews that I recognize and identify with instantly, and I do not find it among Gentiles. When I walk into a Jewish store and talk to a Jewish salesman, we already know each other. When I see a Jewish woman sitting thirty rows back in a church, we know each other. There is a very tangible feeling of "I've been there too, brother" that passes between Jews, right through the skin.

Perhaps the comparison of the Jewish and Gentile communities is meaningless; there are something like four billion Gentiles in the world and some fourteen million Jews. The Jews are inbred, while, over the millennia, the Gentiles are very mixed. There are many times fewer "kinds" of Jews than Gentiles, and they have shared a common history.

But whatever makes for that feeling of intense relationship, it does exist, and almost any Jew can testify to it. (They do not always *want* to testify to it; many Jews, remembering Hitler, consider it dangerous to be identified with a Jewish "type." Many think it best to keep Jewish characteristics under wraps in order not to call any attention to the community. They have a healthy fear of being separated from others because they are Jews, and who can blame them?)

The Jews take care of their women and children. They value education and position. They wish to lead successful lives in a worldly way, and they are strivers. They have a low divorce rate, a high earning rate, a deep respect for well-ordered, well-disciplined life-styles. They eat carefully and prepare their foods painstakingly, even those who do not keep the kosher laws. As a group, they live long and enjoy good health. They assimilate into any culture with a patience and skill born of long experience. Jews make good Americans, good Europeans, good Israelis, or whatever they have to be under some circumstance of emigration or downright fleeing.

Jews do not make very good Communists, it might be said, since those individuals running world Communism tend to tramp on individual rights, and there the Jew invariably draws the line.

Where the Jew is allowed to function in full freedom, as in the United States, he makes quite a success. A recent survey of religious-ethnic groups in the United States, conducted by the National Opinion Research Center, showed that the Jews are the most prosperous single group of religious-ethnic Americans. The Jewish average annual family income was $13,340, according to the study. Anglo-Saxon Protestants averaged $10,354, and Baptists, "the country's poorest whites," averaged $8,693. Many other groups were cited, but the Jews easily exceeded them all in income.

In length of education, the same study found the Jews to lead again (a correlation between length of education and income was expected). The Jews averaged 14 years of schooling; the general national average for whites was 11.1 years.†

It would be curious to see if the income of Hebrew Christians is somewhat less than that of unsaved Jews. Probably it is, the work of taking the Gospel being what it is, and the Scriptures concede that the children of the world are more shrewd than God's children in the ways of the world. Jewish Christians, likely as not, seem to lose some of their zeal for taking the world by storm when they come into the Kingdom that is not of this world.

And that is a relief, I can tell you. I could never have fulfilled my community's expectations of me, I suppose; but with God, not only are all things possible, but some things are not worth worrying about.

Jewish orphanages, senior citizens' homes, care for immigrants, and other community services are traditionally fine, and the community can be counted on for contributions to support these worthy endeavors. Jewish immigrants from Russia, who are beginning to turn up in this country, get special attention and good care as they assimilate into

†Study quoted in *Moneysworth* magazine, Dec. 22, 1975, p. 1.

the Jewish community. One of them wrote to me recently, "I have never had so many people care so much about me, although I had been called 'Comrade' for many years" (It is interesting to consider that we rarely see any *non-Jewish* Russian immigrants. The 250 million Russian Gentiles are doomed to their communistic fate. Some of them may like it, and some not; but it is a sure thing that they cannot leave it. But the Jews have fought and lobbied for the release of their own, and they are accomplishing that. Russian Gentiles who leave are called "defectors." Jews are just called "emigrants." It is a great tribute to the Jewish community everywhere, tiny as it is, that it can have this much effect on international political policies. However they do it, *they do it.*)

Unfortunately, the Jewish community gathers notice that it prefers not to have when it accomplishes such political marvels. In 1974, General George S. Brown delivered some badly phrased remarks about the Jews ("who own, you know, the banks"). He received a reprimand from the president and quite a reaction from the American Jewish community for this careless and inaccurate characterization of an American ethnic group.

For the occasion, *Newsweek* magazine presented the views of Jewish journalist Meg Greenfield, who analyzed the general's comments much along the lines of our discussion here. She also felt that the Jewish community was very capable but was hardly looking for notoriety of the kind given by General Brown. And the truth of the matter is, as she put it, "Jewish control of the banks is about as real a phenomenon as Jewish control of the Archdiocese of New York." She said that such biases were not special to any group; "It was in fact an article of faith in the outer generational reaches of my own Jewish family that Christian men, almost without exception, drank to excess on

Saturday nights and thereafter beat their poor wives sense-
less."

(Writer Greenfield doubtless means "Gentile" when she
says "Christian." It is doubtful that her family meant to
say that men who follow Jesus Christ drink and beat their
wives. But as there *are some* non-Jewish men who drink
and beat their wives, Christians get the credit. It is really
just the nomenclature that is at fault here, but when you
say to a Jew, "Become a Christian," might he not think,
"And spend every Saturday night in a bar?")

The journalist sums up accurately what is actually the
Jewish position on even being recognized as Jews, let alone
controlling banks:

> The postwar exit of American Jews from the "closet" and
> their exuberant public assumption of concern for over-
> seas Jews has coincided with a kind of ethnic frankness
> boom, so that "Jewishness" is now one common currency
> of TV comedy, of political and literary discourse. I will
> confess that it makes me nervous as a cat; and in this I
> know I'm not alone. For behind what must look to General
> Brown like an excess of self-confidence and even cultural
> imperialism, there is a bottomless reservoir of edginess
> and doubt.‡

The Jews, Greenfield sums up, "are too wary, too un-
trusting, too scarred and too certain of their ultimate alone-
ness to tell the General Browns of this world what is really
on their mind."

So, compared to other religious-ethnic groups, there
exists in this America a better-educated, higher-earning,
more comfortably assimilated people who are virtually
afraid to be known as such. They take care of their own
business, their own wives and children and orphans and

‡Meg Greenfield, "The General and the Jews," *Newsweek* 84(De-
cember 9, 1974):43.

old people; they work for the freedom of their less fortunate brethren overseas; and they tirelessly support and fight for the State of Israel. But they fear any hint of slander as if it were a death penalty in itself, because so often it has been.

It is possible that the Jews fear what they think of as Christianity more than they fear another holocaust like the one in Germany. Under dictators with their reigns of horror, the people just grow tougher and are less likely to give up the special bonds that unite them. The Jews outlived Hitler and Stalin, though terribly reduced in number. But they think they would not outlive "conversion" to "another faith." They think, remember, that Christianity is something other than Judaism, and that a Jew will change into something non-Jewish if he follows his Messiah.

In their fear of Christianity, they tend to look down on it. This has almost been a tradition. Aversion toward the Messiah and His followers is more or less a protective device, not really prejudice. Jewish law precludes religious prejudice.

Reading about the lives of past Hebrew Christians, I came upon a shocking document, more or less an obituary, following the death of a Rabbi Isaac Lichtenstein. Rabbi Lichtenstein maintained his calling in Christ and his congregation near Budapest, Hungary, until his death on October 16, 1909. The Yiddish newspaper *Allgemeine Judische Zeitung* dealt harshly with this saint, even in death. The article explains his mission adequately:

> Yesterday the former Reform Rabbi of Tapio Szele, I. Lichtenstein—may his name be blotted out!—was buried here. While still Rabbi, he was in the service of the soul-entrapping mission. From the Jewish pulpit he proclaimed the foundation doctrines of Christianity, and wrote a pamphlet in which he invited the Jews to recognize the

Founder of the Christian religion. Not until the scandal
had lasted a long time did the Reform Rabbinate of Budapest succeed in inducing the representatives of the community of Tapio Szele, composed for the most part of
relatives or friends of Lichtenstein, to demand his dis-
missal, in order that he should withdraw from the Rabbinate.

Since that time the old apostate has lived in Budapest
on money supplied him by English missionary societies,
because he lent his name to missionary purposes. He was
not, however, formally baptized, and thus this "deceiver
and misleader" was buried in the cemetery of the Reform
Synagogue of Budapest. "The name of the wicked shall
rot."§

This touching story of a rabbi who pursued the strange
and difficult ministry of preaching the New Testament
from the Orthodox Jewish pulpit illustrates the vehemence,
and perhaps the fear, of the tightly bonded Jewish community toward an "apostate" in their midst. Members of the
Jewish community, then and now, are well aware of the
Hebrew Christians among them, and they demonstrate in
many ways that they prefer the "General Browns." Doubtless many people became engaged in dialogues with Rabbi
Lichtenstein, probably not unlike those dialogues in my
letters, but the community ultimately had room for him
only in the Reform Synagogue cemetery. (And then only
because he had omitted formal baptism. I was baptized in
the Jordan River near the Sea of Galilee and will definitely
not be buried in a Jewish cemetery. A Jew may be a thief,
a pagan, or a murderer, but he is finally laid to rest with
his fathers in a Jewish cemetery (2 Kings 21:16-18). But

§Translated in *When Jews Face Christ*, by Henry Einspruch (New
York: American Board of Missions to the Jews, 1932). The term *Reform*,
applied to Rabbi Lichtenstein, was an intended insult. He was an Orthodox rabbi.

if he has been baptized into the Christian Church, the law holds that he may *not* be buried with Jewish ancestors.)

It is fair to say about the case of the rabbi of Budapest that he publicly bucked strong Orthodox tradition. The rabbinate simply *had* to recoil from such a demonstration. The Orthodox are very severe in their application of the Law to the community, and doubtless strong pressure was brought to bear against the affronts of Isaac Lichtenstein. It is also fair to say that Rabbi Lichtenstein was supported by his *own* congregation, even to the extent of there being cases of salvation among them.

Modern Conservative and Reform communities would likely not be quite so strict in such an instance. The Conservatives, with their tolerance of both wings, and the Reform, with their live-and-let-live philosophy, might have quietly put "the old apostate" to rest in some neutral ground without editorializing about his career.

But the Orthodox today still abhor the Jewish Christians. They sometimes hold funerals for living children and grandchildren (and parents and grandparents) who "go over to the enemy." This is not even vaguely scriptural, but it is practiced as a warning to those who would even contemplate Christ. The Reverend Charles Halff, who broadcasts nationally on "The Christian Jew Hour," a syndicated radio program, was such a case. He came to the Messiah in his late teens, and his Orthodox family was appalled. His grandmother took him to her bank and had her life savings, eighty-five thousand dollars, laid out before him on a table so that he could choose between the cash and Christ (he chose Christ). The family then held an actual funeral without a body, and Charles was considered dead. He left the city and did not see his family for some fifteen years, during which time his ministry for the Messiah grew in importance. At the end of that period, he went home unannounced. His mother opened the door when he knocked, looked at him briefly, and then shut the door in his face. He left his home again for the last time.

I have suffered no such ostracism from my own family, who are mostly Conservative and Reform. The application of this hard law varies from family to family, so that there are even some forgiving Orthodox Jews, in this regard, to be found nowadays. But this is far from saying that they *like* the idea of a Hebrew Christian in their midst.

Recently I had a rare opportunity to confront a group of some forty Conservative Jews in a program where they chose to hear me out. I was actually invited to give my testimony at a neighborhood *Havurah* (fellowship) where Conservative Jewish couples gathered once a month. I was sent a friendly invitation and also telephoned. And I was assured that I would have a chance to speak and answer questions before the group. The Havurah was looking at all sides of Judaism in a succession of meetings, and they did not omit that bad brother, Hebrew Christianity.

I took along my wife, "the Gentile," for moral support, and she sat among the assembled skeptics, looking for all the world like any good Jew's wife. I also took along a selection of my books, not expecting that merchandise to move very fast, and displayed them on a table in front of the crowd. (This was psychologically very important. I wanted to demonstrate in front of everyone that I was not going to hide my allegiance to the Lord for the sake of being accepted by the group. Probably some of them thought before I arrived, "He probably won't say anything antagonistic around here; he'll say, 'Why don't we all be friends?'" Well, I did not want to say anything antagonistic if it could be helped, but I was going to say who the Messiah was, loud and clear, and I did that by putting my books in plain view. One glance at a title like *How Did a*

Fat, Balding, Middle-Age Jew Like You Become a Jesus Freak? or *Jesus, the Jew's Jew* reveals pretty much where I stand.)

I was right about the books. I did not sell a single one. But I had laid out my business cards, and seven of them were mysteriously missing after the meeting.

A friendly rabbi was present, seated at the end of the room where the speaker was to hold forth. I had been told about this only on the day of the Havurah; presumably someone decided at the last moment that it might be a good idea for a rabbi to be present to monitor what the "stranger" had to say. I was introduced to the rabbi at the outset and learned that he had formerly taught at a local Jewish academy, so I knew that I was confronting a scholarly and academically prepared rabbi.

The setting, I should say, was the living room of a private home, not a synagogue meeting room, and the members of the Havurah were seated informally, mostly on the floor. The atmosphere was casual and, in view of the circumstances, quite agreeable.

The debate (for that is what the program had now become, with the addition of the rabbi to the proceedings) began with me giving my testimony. I told it simply, emphasizing how my life had changed since I had accepted the Messiah. I stressed that I felt more, not less, Jewish in my heart. I devoted a good part of my opening time to citing a dozen powerful prophecies pointing to Jesus as the Messiah, wanting to get the rabbi on solid, scriptural ground. I read the Scriptures word for word and explained their fulfillments in the gospels. I reminded the assembly that I was reading from *our* Holy Bible. I did not quote the New Testament at all, the fulfillments of such prophecies as the virgin birth, Bethlehem, and so forth, being widely known anyway. I challenged the rabbi to refute the prophecies.

The rabbi discussed purely cultural Judaism, confusing traditional feasts with scriptural feasts and the words of sages with the Word of God. I do not want to demean what the rabbi said, as it was a valuable, sincere, and penetrating estimation of the Judaism he knew. It included, of course, the Jewish aversion to the Carpenter of Nazareth as the Messiah, but it brought out subtleties of modern Jewish life that seemed to demonstrate that I, the Hebrew Christian, greatly undervalue Judaism. The rabbi barely dealt with the prophecies I cited, saying only, "The Scriptures are needful of interpretation." He stressed that proper Judaism is a legal system and that the Law is being substantially kept today, the Law being quite "flexible." He said he was sure he could find the scriptural justification for any modern Jewish practice, given about three days with the Torah. He said that the Messiah was not to come to save His people from their sins but to rule the world. Judaism does not hold that people are born sinful, the rabbi stated, and thus does not teach that they need special salvation.

I took up his points one by one, with great care, in order to honor the idea that he believed what he was saying. I did not imagine for a moment that either my audience or debating opponent was being insincere or trying to offend me (although one question I was asked during my testimony was "How much do the Christians pay you for each convert you bring them from your own people?"). The atmosphere was highly charged, but I could see that all present were trying to find common ground. The only time I myself objected to the proceedings was when one member stated that attitudes like mine (supposedly defamatory to Judaism) "have killed one million Jews"! On the other side, there was one strong objection. A woman, on the verge of sobbing, leaped to her feet and told me off in a shaky voice; then she stormed out of the house altogether. She said pointedly, "The only valuable part of this wasted evening is that we have been able to hear the wisdom of the rabbi!"

In my refutation of the rabbi's points, I stayed entirely in the Scriptures, always quoting them. I had brought two Bibles, including a separate New Testament, so that my listeners could see when I was quoting the "Christian" Bible and when the "Jewish" Bible. On the rabbi's point about the Scriptures being "needful" of interpretation, I asked him (and the listeners) if there was really anything unclear about Micah's reference to Bethlehem (a Hebrew word meaning "house of bread") or Isaiah's reference to the virgin birth, or any number of other verses that I quoted. I asked if they thought God had really intended to give the chosen people, for their guidance and teaching, a book they could not understand. I said that I personally found the Scriptures quite clear, though sometimes requiring meditation.

I repeated several of the most obvious of the prophecies that I had cited earlier and that the rabbi had not dealt with, and I insisted on knowing why God had included them in His Word. I reminded the listeners that I was giving only a few of some three hundred quite clear Messianic prophecies and that if anyone wished, I could run through them all (no one expressed that wish).

I asked how many present were keeping the "613 Laws," or if anyone present, including the rabbi, even *knew* them all. If Judaism is a legal system, I asked, why don't the people know the Law? And if the Law was so "flexible," as the rabbi had asserted, why did God keep on pronouncing the death penalty in connection with transgressions (and I read several such statements from the Scripture).

I said that I would give him three days to find in the Scripture that Rosh Hashanah was the New Year. I gave him my card. I did not expect to hear from him in three days, and in fact I have never heard anything from him again. (My gesture of picking up my card from the book table to present to the rabbi was more to show the Havurah members where they could find my card on the way out than to seriously challenge the rabbi on a point he could not win. As I said above, people did note where they could get my phone number, and seven of the forty availed themselves of it. Sincerely, I would not be surprised to hear from those seven persons years from now—even on their deathbeds.)

I read Isaiah 53 to the rabbi and the crowd in connection with whether the Messiah was to come to save His people from sin ("He was wounded for our transgressions, he was bruised for our iniquities . . . with his stripes we are healed"). If the Jews have no concept of being born in sin, I asked, why did King David say, "In sin did my mother conceive me" (Psalm 51:5)?

The Messiah was indeed to rule the world, I agreed, and certainly will do so. Obviously His comings are two and separate. I explained how the Lord came as a Lamb and, in the future, is to come as a Lion, and why. I told them that I certainly sympathized with the ancient, and modern, Jewish hope of a powerful Deliverer who would at last put a stop, once and for all, to the persecution and abuse of the chosen people. But God's plan first involved an intercessory mission and *then* a kingly one. I pointed out that the whole idea for Jews now was to line up with the Messiah in His intercessory capacity and be cleansed and ready for the Kingdom to come.

They were probably a bit surprised to hear so reasonable

and Jewish-centered an argument for receiving the "Gentile" Saviour. He was *ours*, I continually reminded them, and they nodded.

After my "rebuttal," the rabbi excused himself and said he had to be going. He left the gathering, and the hostess suggested that the group might adjourn for refreshments and conversation. My wife and I were strictly avoided by some of the participants but sought out by some others.

The informal hour went somewhat the same way as the preceding "debate," with the members of the Havurah talking to me about modern Jewish custom, and me talking to them about the Bible. There were intelligent questions, but certainly no one wanted to make any sort of decision for Christ. The ladies seemed to want to examine my wife as the culprit who must have cunningly drawn away one of the chosen men (I had given her the credit when I presented my testimony).

Worlds of new understanding opened to me when I was introduced to the hostess' daughter and prospective son-in-law; I suddenly realized that the young man was not Jewish. The hostess, who had of course donated her home to this unusual exercise in the first place, must have had an ax to grind, and it was a difficult one—her daughter wanted to marry a Gentile. I watched the young man carefully, and he smiled perceptibly at me. I determined later that he was a Christian, committed to the Lord, and in no small way responsible for the whole evening. I took it upon myself to assure the hostess that she was probably in for more blessings than she anticipated in her daughter's impending marriage. I tried to indicate to her, without being too familiar, that her daughter had chosen the best of all possible Gentiles, but she acknowledged this only vaguely. She had apparently been willing to listen to what a Hebrew Christian thought, but she was not about to value his opinion on what she must have considered a real tragedy in her personal life.

The talk seemed to go on and on after the main event of the evening, and obviously the tense debate had stirred up much controversy. My wife was especially effective with the women, simply assuring them that one's life does not go awry when he receives the Messiah, and that the Christian life is worth looking into. I myself wrestled with the inevitable questions about various Christian failings, always answering that the only perfect Christian we have seen ascended to His Father long ago.

I only wished that the rabbi would have been able to remain for some informal conversation. He was the one, more than anyone else present, who would be able to see my point. There was no knowledge of the Bible to speak of among the audience, but the rabbi surely knew that the Scriptures I applied were in the Word, and perhaps he had had a new insight or two about the Messiah.

But maybe that is why he left. I may hear from him someday.

Rabbis come to the Messiah fairly readily, it may surprise some Christians to know. It is because their hearts are by and large spiritual. The Orthodox, who respect the Bible and something of the supernatural aspects of God's plans, are the most likely to see the light, and, indeed, some striking examples of Christian faith have been seen among the rabbinate, as in the case of Isaac Lichtenstein of Budapest. The American Board of Missions to the Jews, the largest of the Jewish evangelism organizations, was founded by an Orthodox rabbi who had come to his Messiah.

But Conservative and Reform rabbis are much less likely to give the Gospel a fair hearing, and some of the Reform frankly admit to being disbelievers in God. They consider the spiritual aspects of life—such as love, beauty, and sacrifice—to be entirely worldly, being just so many psychological ramifications of human personality, and they think secular leaders are competent to guide religious flocks.

I recorded a brief conversation between a witnessing Christian and a Conservative rabbi at a *briss*, the Jewish ceremony of circumcision held on the eighth day after birth. It was an unusual enough *briss* to start with, since the parents, unknown to the rabbi, were both Christians. The father was a faithful and scholarly Gentile Christian, and the mother a Jewish Christian. They wanted to have a *briss* to celebrate the ancient way of admitting a Jewish male into the Abrahamic covenant (faith, not circumcision, as Paul pointed out, admits any man into that covenant today). The parents were not keeping the Law, of course, but merely felt that the biblical custom was more to their liking than a mere hospital circumcision.

They also desired an opportunity to witness to a rabbi, so they retained one for the ceremony. The rabbi would not have officiated if he had fully understood the position of both parents in Christ, but here was a situation where the technicalities of the Jewish understanding of Christ worked to the advantage of the Christians. The husband did specify that he was a Christian, which to the rabbi simply meant "Gentile." The wife was Jewish, but the rabbi would not have taken her belief in the Messiah seriously, since, in his thinking, the Messiah had not as yet arrived. Thus, the rabbi conceived, in his various biases, that he was dealing with a mere mixed marriage in which the strong will of the Jewish wife had prevailed and a proper circumcision ceremony was to be held. That had happened plenty of times before, and the rabbi was glad to oblige. Here was a mixed marriage, he thought, where the Jew in the family had prevailed. So things go in the Jewish community.

The circumcision was mercifully brief (I had to hold the baby since I was the godfather), and none of the women, or men, fainted, as occasionally happens during this mixed blessing of a Jewish custom. Little John came through his introduction to Abraham with very little fuss, and we all complimented the *mohel* (circumcisor) on his skill. The rabbi did the minor operation himself; many rabbis perform this simple surgery, occasionally even for hospitals.)

The interesting part came afterwards, during the social time that inevitably follows any Jewish worship. The conversation I referred to above was between the father of the child and the rabbi, and it concerned the father's name. He noticed that the rabbi pronounced his name in English, but his wife's name in Hebrew, and he asked how he might get a Jewish name.

The rabbi said, "Well, why don't you just convert to Judaism?"

"Would I have to give up my belief in Jesus as the Jewish Messiah?" the young father replied, skillfully witnessing with his question.

The rabbi's answer, and these are his exact words, sums up the Conservative Jewish position on Christ, if not the position of all Jewry:

"Certainly! That is the one thing we can't tolerate. We ask certain questions of converts, and the first one is, 'Do you give up your belief in a Trinity and your belief in a personal God?'"

The father was not giving up any such beliefs, and the rabbi departed.

It may come as a shock to many Christians that the rabbi's conversion procedure insists upon the renouncing of a personal God. The aversion to the Trinity on the part of the modern Jews is understandable, but most Christians think the Jews revere the concept of a personal God. This is not the case. Prayer in Judaism is practiced in groups and discouraged as an individual exercise, though it is done in private anyway. Ten men must assemble to make up a *minyan* (prayer quorum), and certain ceremonies require the presence of a Levite. (I have served as the Levite sanctifying a prayer group on many occasions, though since I have become a Christian, the very people who previously respected my high calling now say, "You can't prove your lineage." I expect to get future calls to preside over prayers from Jewish people who merely look up my very "Levite name" in the phone book, and I will go, and I will pray with them.)

Many Jewish people deny that God is impersonal, since it sounds wrong (and *is* wrong, considering the Scriptures), but I have it on good authority that personal prayer to a personal God is to be discouraged in the Jewish community. I learned this from a highly placed rabbi to whom I was witnessing in Jerusalem. Not two miles away, devout Jewish people lined the Wailing wall, pressing little pieces of paper, on which they had written notes to God, into the cracks in the stone.

What I call "the Jewish mystique" goes on and on—traditions, customs, a warmhearted (sometimes wholly inaccurate) respect for God and His Word, a perfectly human amalgam of odds and ends of apostasy so typical of this people for the past four thousand years (see Rom 10:14). Some of them love their own people with such an intensity that the community, not the worship of God, becomes Judaism for them. Some of them try to hide from the community or stay on its edges in order to avoid the next persecution. Some of them love Israel enough to emigrate to it and take on the difficult lives of pioneers and soldiers. Some wish only to forget Zionism and all its present problems and "feel personally threatened by Zionism and by what we [Jews] consider to be the backward, tribal, undemocratic, indisputable objective of political Zionism—the ingathering of all Jews into the state of Israel."||

The Jewish mystique is love of family and community, dogged respect for rabbi and synagogue, appreciation of fine food and rich humor, the honoring of women and their protection and well-being, the education of the young, the tender care for the old, the gallant opposition to the "General Browns," the genuine concern for Iron-Curtain Jewry and Jews everywhere, the love of the land of Israel, and the ever present, generation-after-generation aversion to all things non-Jewish, including the "head Gentile," Jesus Christ.

But the Jewish mystique is also the inaccuracy of Torah interpretation, the keeping of pointless laws, the dread of the whole world of Gentiles, the lack of spiritual comprehension of the rabbis, the ongoing apostasy of millennia, and aversion to all things they consider non-Jewish, including the Messiah, Jesus Christ.

People misinterpret the King James Version of the Bible in its usage of "peculiar" in God's statement that He had chosen to Himself a peculiar people. God meant a "special" or "unique" or "separated" people. But after some experience with the Jewish people, many Bible readers smile at "peculiar" and misinterpret it.

Or do they?

||Letter to the editor, *Time* 106(November 24, 1975).

5

The Local Church Versus the Local Synagogue

Jews are unimpressed with churches; and they feel that their own worship is more acceptable to God.

In this section I have drawn heavily upon the knowledge and memories of my friend Dr. Thomas S. McCall, a learned missionary to the Jews who holds a doctor of theology degree in Old Testament studies. Dr. McCall has participated in quite a bit of authentic Jewish worship in various synagogues during the outworkings of his unique ministry. I have also included my own recollections and experiences.

Tom waxed very eloquent in our interview about his experiences with Jewish worship. He cited a very noticeable feeling of spiritual superiority among the Jews, and he has heard a host of reasons for it.

"Once I was witnessing to a Jew and he asked me, 'Why should I settle for a piece of bread when I can have the whole loaf?' Judaism represented for him 'the whole loaf.' I checked this objection with another missionary, and he said I should have countered, 'Why settle for a loaf when you can have the whole bakery?'"

Jews do not believe that Christianity offers the whole bakery, because to them it is simply inferior religion. First and foremost, they feel that the Jews have direct access to God while Christians are obliged to go through a Mediator

(Christ). Then they think that the outworkings of Christian faith are not as impressive as those of Judaism; the Christian heritage, family relationships, community closeness, and "culture" seem to them not as effective as they are in the world of Judaism.

They make the accusation that Christianity, with all of its doctrines of forgiveness and love, produces persecutors. This thinking, Tom elaborated, involves blaming the evangelical church for such crimes as the Inquisition, in which so many Jews were tortured and executed. But such sources as *Foxe's Christian Martyrs of the World* show that Evangelicals received the same treatment at the hands of the inquisitors. Unfortunately, though, however far from the Gospel the persecutors of Jews were through the ages, they carried that same cross. The Jews are being asked a great deal, under the circumstances, to make fine distinctions among heresies.

An Israeli government official said, "The only nation that everyone expects to act in a Christian way is Israel!"

On the other hand, say the Jews, Jews are not persecutors, and history fairly well bears this out. Depending on the point of view, one has to go back to biblical times to see conquering Jewish armies. Then again, the Jewish nation has been weak and dispersed and hardly had the opportunity to persecute. Still, Palestinians today constantly accuse the Israelis of persecution.

Tom points out an example of intrafaith persecution among the Jews in the case of the Hebrew Christians. These are regarded by the Orthodox at least as traitors. The term applied to them in Yiddish is *Meshumed* (deserter).

Finally, the Jews proudly embrace "deed, not creed" religion. The feeling is that the Jew is busy doing his good works toward God while the Christian sleeps. The Jewish community abounds with orphanages, child care centers, senior citizens homes, and the like, while the Christian is pictured as relaxing in his benign gift of salvation. (The Jews, of course, do not subscribe to New Testament pronouncements about "faith not works"; rather, they reflect the spirit of Mosaic Law, where external performance was vital.)

It is terribly hard to make judgments about these things, and our purpose here is not to discern right and wrong. Such matters as "Who is the persecutor?" are emotional issues among men. God settled long ago, in both Testaments, that all men sin.

But we *are* discerning just why the Jews do not want their rightful Messiah, and that has a great deal to do with how they feel about Christianity and Judaism as practiced.

Most Jews and Christians know little about each other's worship practices. But Tom McCall has had the unique experience of standing right at the altar in both kinds of worship. His lifework has been to make a study of both.

And me, well, I am a Jewish Christian.

Concerning the modern synagogue and what is done there, we must bear in mind that there are various Jewish sects, just as there are various Christian sects. Jewish congregations follow one of three major subdivisions—Orthodox, Conservative, and Reformed.

Tom's richest experience with Jewish worship was in the most orthodox of the Orthodox—the storefront synagogue.

These informal but strict congregations abounded in the ghettos of Europe, where space was at a premium. The settings were not fancy, but God and His Law were respected with a zeal hard to find in worship anywhere. The tradition was continued in some sectors in this country, particularly in the big cities where crowded conditions must have reminded the immigrant Jews of hard but reverent times gone by.

Tom's experience was in Los Angeles. He was pursuing his graduate studies at Talbot Theological Seminary, and he was eager to observe the chosen people at their worship.

Nobody shakes your hand or gives you a visitor's card when you enter a storefront synagogue. In fact, they don't even look up. Despite all of his Gentile appearance, Tom was able just to take a seat and participate in the goings-on.

At the end of his first service, Tom was asked if he would kindly shut off the lights. The idea was that the Orthodox Jew can do no work at all on the Sabbath—not even operate a light switch—and a Gentile was pressed into service. Normally a member of the congregation would go out into the street and stop a passerby; but since Tom was handy, he was like a gift from God.

Tom was delighted to be what is called in Yiddish the *Shabbas Goy* (the Sabbath Gentile). After all, it gave him a certain standing in the congregation and guaranteed him entrance each Saturday morning.

However, he lost his job after two weeks, because he was able to pray along with the austere worshipers. The congregation prayed in Hebrew and conversed in Yiddish, and Tom's Hebrew was adequate to follow the prayers and participate to an acceptable degree. This made him more of a prayer partner than a true *Shabbas Goy*, and the men of the congregation felt that they themselves might be defiled for permitting a prayer partner to do the work on the Sabbath.

"It was a kind of acceptance," muses Tom.

(Actually, Tom's Hebrew was excellent in terms of what modern Hebrew is. He had studied with the up-to-date scholars at Talbot, under Dr. Charles Lee Feinberg, and he pronounced the sharp, clear Israeli Hebrew of today.

The congregation pronounced Ashkenazik Hebrew, the regional accent of Europe, which is heavily influenced by Yiddish and by localized sounds. I myself speak Ashkenazik as a result of studying with European refugees in Hebrew School as a boy, and I am simply not understood in Tel Aviv. You can see that there is more to Jewish worship than meets the eye!)

So Tom became what we might call half of a full-fledged member of the little congregation in the store in Los Angeles. He was faithful in attendance, an important precept of Jewish worship, and he joined the thirty to forty members each Sabbath. (The women of the congregation sat behind a high opaque screen where they could be heard but not seen.)

Each Saturday morning for about a year, Tom would do the relatively strenuous worship procedure, which consisted of some two hours of selections from the Psalms, a half hour each from the Law and the prophets, a sermonette, and hymns.

There was a dramatic moment early in Tom's year concerning the reading of the Torah. In each service the holy Torah, or the Pentateuch, is brought forth from the Ark for the reading of the Law. It is a most reverent act to open the curtains and doors of the Ark and produce the beautiful scrolls that bear God's Law. All stand in sacred respect at the sight of the open Ark, and many introductory prayers are given before the reading of the Law commences.

It is a great honor to read aloud from the Torah, and in Tom's congregation five men per week were selected for this office. They would invariably tremble as they approached the Holy Word.

Well, in the natural order of things, men make mistakes. One Sabbath morning Tom was chosen as one of the five readers!

There was a sudden hush of astonishment as the leader gestured to Tom. (The little congregation did not have a rabbi but used leaders, in the sense of elders). Everyone was aghast, including the former *Shabbas Goy,* at the prospect of Reverend McCall reading the Law. Then the people found their voices, and there was much buzzing.

Inevitably Tom heard, "No, no, he's a Goy," in West Coast English among the panicky worshipers.

Tom was going to decline in any case, since the reading of the Torah required exacting Hebrew and a style familiar only to experienced Torah chanters. But, before he could, the honor was quickly passed along to someone else.

Otherwise, the year passed uneventfully for Tom, and he managed to establish fellowship with some of the congregation. The worship should not be made to sound unfriendly by any means, since synagogues are invariably warm and heartening places. Tom remembers the hymn singing, which ended each worship service, as a time of rare spiritual fellowship with participation by all the members.

Tom was even able to witness to two of the congregation's members as the year passed. The song leader was a young Israeli engineer, deeply dedicated to Israel and engaged in studying American long-distance irrigation methods for use in the Holy Land. He was interested in the Feather River Project, which brings water from Northern California to the dry Southern areas of the state, in a rough parallel to the Galilee-Negev situation in Israel. He and another member of the group were willing to hear Tom out on his scriptural views.

The witnessing did not bear fruit in this case, mainly because of the entirely different opinions about what the Scriptures mean. The Jews held that the Bible was God's Word indeed, but that it contained "many messiahs." They did not know the meanings of the Scriptures very well, since they were accustomed to reading the Hebrew without translation. Tom was disturbed to find that many of the congregation had been trained only to *read* the Scriptures and could not translate them. And in this new English-speaking world the meanings were slipping away, rather like the situation with the Latin Mass.

The attitude toward Jesus was negative. Not only was He not the Messiah, they felt, but He was not worth talking about. Good fellowship does not always succeed in sharing the faith.

Tom had other interesting experiences along the way in his training to become like a Jew for the sake of the Jews. Also in Los Angeles, he came across a Conservative congregation that had quite a witnessing and converting program! He attended a meeting that was "evangelical" or, rather, outreaching in nature, on behalf of the synagogue. The synagogue operated a school of instruction in the Jewish faith, mainly conceived to ease the problems of "mixed marriage." The Gentile partner of such marriages was strongly encouraged to take the instruction and convert to Judaism for practical reasons, but others of the community were welcome, too.

In his later career in Dallas, Tom was able to strike up a good relationship with an Orthodox rabbi. That rabbi invited Tom to inspect his synagogue's *mikva* (ritual bath). The bath was utilized in conversions and in certain purification rites preceding special events. Realizing that Tom was a Baptist, the rabbi assumed correctly that he would be very interested in this curious parallel between the faiths.

My own experiences were more with the Conservative and Reformed sectors of Judaism. I did occasionally visit the local Orthodox synagogue, which was a full-sized, mag-

nificent building, and I marveled at the differences from
my own Conservative synagogue. In that Orthodox synagogue the podium was in the middle of the huge worship
room, like the arrangement of a boxing arena. The women
sat upstairs, as usual, out of sight and mind. The services
were utterly inexplicable to me. They seemed to consist
of a few privileged men on the dais, virtually reading to
themselves out of the Torah, while the rest made out as
well as they could.

Of course, I failed to appreciate the finer points of the
worship, but my total experience with synagogues was in
my boyhood. I pretty much quit attending after my Bar
Mitzvah at age thirteen.

My own congregation was a large one, and the synagogue was auditorium-style, with the podium at the front
and the women seated with their families. There were
choir lofts from which issued music so fine that it had a
permanent effect on my life. I think I went to music school
because of the inspiration of that splendid music. Our
synagogue paid the singers and attracted many fine pro-
fessionals. I still have trouble settling for church music (at
the risk of sounding like one of those Jewish "superiors").

The synagogue provided a Hebrew school and Sunday
school, fully staffed and reasonably effective for transfer-
ring the difficult concepts of the faith. I learned my Hebrew pretty well and my Jewish history and traditions. I
especially remember the unmitigated joy in 1948 when we
recovered our promised land; our Sunday school class went
wild.

And I can never forget my rabbi, who was much more
than a clergyman to me. My mother instilled in me a
worshipful respect for that fine man, and to me he looked
as though he were right next to God at all times. I would
almost shudder to see his white satin *yarmulke* set regally

on his silver hair as he sermonized with the virtual voice of God.

But as far the actual worship went, I was almost completely lost. Although much of our service was in English, in the Conservative tradition, and although I faithfully attended Hebrew school, where we practiced the Hebrew portions, I just could never get with it. I would stand when everybody stood, sing when everybody sang, and I kissed the Torah as it passed in the aisle. But I never knew what was really going on.

Most of the meaning for me was in the place and its artifacts. It was a marvelous building with every wall painted in murals, and heroic chandeliers and pillars everywhere. It was dark and warm, trimmed in heavy woods and gold, and I thrilled to its very appearance. Beside me on the wall were what I called the "death lights"—little light bulbs beside the names of honored ancestors; the lights would shine on the anniversaries of their deaths. I studied those names, which were engraved on beautiful gold plaques, to pass the time, and I said secret prayers for those in whose memory the lights were lit each Sabbath.

There was one part of the service that was clear to me—the mourners' prayer. The Rabbi would intone, "Let those who mourn now rise," and a few members would stand for the overwhelmingly tragic and beautiful chant for the dead. I led that chant on the morning of my Bar Mitzvah.

The Jews have no clear concept of a heaven or an afterlife. My mother spoke of "the other world" where *her* mother was, and once when a bird flew into our house, she thought it might have been a message from the other world. But the idea of an afterlife varies with almost each Jew. There is a feeling that the dead ought to be prayed for, particularly on the first anniversary of their deaths, and it is almost a foreboding feeling, as though the dead one were in a kind of purgatory depending on the prayers of the living. But again, this was the feeling *I* had from *my* congregation. It would vary elsewhere.

I remember a moment in my synagogue worship times that would serve to illustrate the very real reverence of the Jew for the Law. There was a day when they neglected to fully close the Ark. The Torah had been read and replaced, and the inner wooden doors were closed, but the curtains remained open, simply forgotten by the leaders on the podium. The ark was behind them, and they failed to notice as the service went on.

It was an all-day service on a high holy day, I recall. People had been standing, of course, when the Ark was open, but now they looked at one another, shrugged, and sat down, assuming that the forgotten curtains would not make a difference. All of us sat down except for one very aged man near me. He remained standing by the hour, and my heart went out to him.

He was noticed, of course, but not from the podium. Individual worshipers may stand for different reasons during the worship, and it was a big congregation.

He began losing strength and was fairly leaning on the pew in front of him after a while. But in no case would he be seated while the curtains of the Ark were parted.

Finally an elder on the podium noticed the curtains and closed them. The old man stood a moment longer, as if to say, "If my God requires it, I can go on," and then sat heavily. He was exhausted.

He has stuck in my mind all these years; I can still see that stoic, old face. He knew the traditional Law, and he obeyed it to the letter.

That could never have happened in the Reformed temple. Reformed Judaism, or "Reform" as it is called, is closely comparable to liberal Protestantism. Its emphasis is on social matters and heritage rather than on worship. The services are entirely in English, and God is sort of a concept rather than a Person.

I had few experiences with it. It was pleasant enough, "worship" being completely understandable, but for me it lacked the pomp and the grandeur of what I had come to think of as a proper approach to God. Reformed synagogues are generally called Temples, though this seems backward from Scripture (one would assume that only the higher forms of the faith would use God's own term).

Reformed Judaism, like liberal Protestantism, has wide appeal, because it requires much less of the adherent than the stricter sects. It tends to attract many Jews who are loathe to leave the faith altogether but are equally loathe to endure the lengthy services and education deemed necessary by Conservative or Orthodox groups.

One might think that with all the apparent similarity between Reformed Judaism and liberal Protestantism, they might someday merge. Perhaps Jews will quietly begin to attend the less demanding churches, and Gentiles will find the Jewish social views palatable. When people living in the same culture embrace similar ideas, doesn't it bring them closer together? Not in this case. There exists a fine but clearly drawn line between all that is Jewish and all that is Gentile, and that is all there is to that.

According to Dr. McCall, this line is even observable within the Christian community, for among Evangelicals there is a distinction between Jews and Gentiles in Christ. This ought not to be, because scripturally "there is neither Jew nor Greek . . . in Christ" (Gal 3:28), but, as he observes, "I live with it every day."

To understand why Jews do not respond to what Christians call "good Christian fellowship," we must understand these underlying biases. First, it is fair to say that

the biases go both ways. The degree to which the local
church feels superior to the local synagogue is the same
degree to which the local synagogue feels superior to the
local church. According to Tom, we have a divided fault.
Both sides observe historic distinctions between the Jew
and the Gentile.

Gentiles, both Christian and unbelieving, tend to believe the ageless negative attitudes: the Jews killed Christ;
they had their chance and muffed it. Jewish stereotypes
still exist in the Gentile mind: every Jew is a penny pincher
or a suspiciously shrewd businessman. Jews are typically
excluded from country clubs and society-page activities;
there are few Jewish debutantes and little Jewish participation in society fund-raising parties and the like. Jews
come to belief in Christ but are seldom seen in Sunday
school or in church. For a "good Christian family" to have
a close relationship with a Jewish family is, in the Christians' view, somehow subtly demeaning.

It should also be said, though, that many Gentile Christians strive to overcome this situation but do not know
quite how to do it.

On the other side of the coin, the Jews may be faulted
for carrying out the enmity of the old Law unnecessarily.

The Law of Moses laid heavy stress on Jewish separate-
ness. God had chosen a people, and He was a jealous God,
He said, and the Jews were not even to make inquiries
about their neighbors' worship. That was truly the spirit
of the thing under the old covenant.

But there has been a lot of water under the bridge since
then. The attitude of Jewish superiority survived well,
even through the ministry of Jesus and on into the New
Testament. Peter casually tells Cornelius, "Ye know how
that it is an unlawful thing for a man that is a Jew to keep
company, or come unto one of another nation; but God

hath shewed me that I should not call any man common or unclean" (Acts 10:28). But the epistles go on to point out, "For he is our peace, who hath made both [Jews and Gentiles] one, and hath broken down the middle wall of partition between us" (Eph 2:14).

Since unbelieving Jews still hold to the Old Testament views of things, the Jewish superiority is still in force for them. But even Hebrew Christians, according to Tom, practice some residue of the old enmity. "They were all raised with it," he points out. The Jew, even the believer, feels ill at ease in the Christian church. He feels outnumbered, vaguely defiled, and, at heart, like a kind of deserter of his people. He senses that the atmosphere in the church does not match his concept of a proper house of worship.

And there is plenty of Gentile stereotyping among the Jews: the Gentile is a drunkard; Gentiles hate Jews; Gentiles are insensitive and lack depth. My father had an expression in Yiddish that meant "for the *Goyim*." New cars were for the *Goyim*. Name-brand clothing was for the *Goyim*. Anything overpriced or inferior in quality was "for the *Goyim*."

We must appreciate that God had once designed actual physical barriers to separate Gentiles and Jews, as in the ancient Temples. The five-foot-high stone wall prohibiting Gentiles from entrance into the Temple area has been found by archaeologists. (And that was not the only segregation. As one proceeded into the Temple area, he came to a wall prohibiting women from going any farther; then all men except the Levites had to stop; then, finally, all Levites except the high priest!)

There certainly were no strollers or curiosity seekers in the old Temples. And the tradition has been continued. Rarely do new people casually enter a synagogue. Normally a new family in the neighborhood is received only

gradually into what is virtually a closed society. While
evangelical churches plead for new members and offer in-
vitations at every service—visitors cards and the like, if not
a spoken invitation—nothing of the kind is done in the
typical synagogue. We were an "in-group" at my synagogue, and even our friends who had passed away joined
us annually via those little death lights.

(But again, policies vary greatly in Judaism. We have
already described Tom's experience with the outreaching
Conservative congregation in Los Angeles.)

Tom's problem, as a missionary to the Jews, is to constantly remind both Jew and Gentile believers that
"through him we both have access by one Spirit unto the
Father" (Eph 2:18). Ideally, God would have the arrangement He depicts in chapter 2 of Ephesians: a holy temple
of Jews and Gentiles together in worship.

And it just does not exist.

God's preference for one body, one bride for Christ, in
the Christian Church has not been achieved.

In a realistic way it has not been achieved, because it
requires men to break old habits almost precious to them.
Jews have never come to church in any numbers, so Gentiles would have to break precedent to receive them. And
the Jews would have to get over the fear of assimilation,
the dreaded loss of Jewish identity.

Actually, at present, things seem to be moving in the
direction of more separation rather than more togetherness
in some sectors of the Church. There is a Hebrew Christian
alliance where Jews may be members but Gentile Christians may only be "associates."

On the other hand, many churches are beginning to have
regularly scheduled "Jewish events," such as Israel and
Prophecy conferences, dinners, and social evenings.

Well, it's a very wide topic with many ramifications. As

to why the Jews do not want their Messiah, our main subject, this comparison of worship styles and differences
between modern peoples throws light on only a fraction of
it. That the Jews do not respond to Christian fellowship is
easy to see. The reasons behind it are more subtle, involving everything from the Mosaic Law to the coming out of
the debutantes.

Before we proceed to some suggestions on witnessing to
the Jews, one solution to the whole dilemma, we should
recognize that Jews do not think of Christians as truly
religious people. Jews are not very likely to embrace a
faith they think is not real or not godly.

And the fact is, the Jews call Christians "Gentiles."

The term *Gentile* as used by the Jew (and by Jesus, Matt
6:32, for example) means simply "unbeliever." To the
average Jew, a Christian is just another variety of unbeliever, comparable to ancient pagans.

Tom says that many Jews think of Christianity as a religion of strange artifacts and practices. All Gentiles, they
say, are idolators in some way or another. Here are the
Christians with their crucifixes and statues and pictures
and holy water—all the typical paraphernalia of pagan
worship—and they ask the Jew to believe that this is what
God wants.

To the Jew, God has to be remote. That is just the essence of God: He is invisible and He brooks no representa-
tions of Himself. Proper worship is a subtle achievement
of following explicitly what one cannot see.

Jesus, then, becomes an artifact to the Jew. Christianity
involves the deification of a mere man. I have actually
heard it put into Yiddish words: "Any *schnook* can worship
a man." To the sincere Christian worshiper, that hurts.
But we are here to help the unbeliever, not judge him.

Another problem is the ruination of the very term *Chris-*

tian, a biblical term for the followers of Christ, the Jewish Messiah. *Christian* means "Christ in one." But the majority of American Gentiles call themselves Christians, and so the Jew is confronted with a tremendous variation of beliefs and non-beliefs gathered under one confusing designation. When a Gentile who is a true believer says, "I am a Christian," his Jewish friend says, "Of course you are; you're not Jewish."

And you know, when all Gentiles become "Christian" in the Jewish mind, the true Christian witness is greatly harmed.

So far, we have confined this discussion to the American Jewish scene. That is where most of my experience has been and where most of the readers of this book will be found. But of course no discussion of Judaism today would be complete without the inclusion of Israel, the rightful home of world Jewry. Israel is, in a very real way, the beating heart of Judaism today, and that is in keeping with God's plan.

Christians are witnessing in Israel, as we will see in the following chapter, and Jesus is at last being taken back to His homeland. The problems in the promised land are myriad as regards the international political situation, and most complex as regards the spiritual situation.

But the Lord came out of Nazareth to gather His Jewish men together and save the nation of Israel. He made a tremendous effort for the chosen people, His brethren. With His disciples, He started a movement in Israel that was to change the world.

He ascended to His Father long ago, but His disciples go on, right where it all started.

6

"Can Any Good Thing Come Out of Nazareth?"

Nathanael was a skeptic. When Philip told him the Messiah had come, he asked wryly, "Can any good thing come out of Nazareth?" (John 1:46, NASB).

Spiritually, Israel has not changed a whole lot in the past two thousand years or so. The same basic divisions of the unique Israeli society that Jesus confronted in His earthly ministry are still to be found there today. Nathanael is alive and well and living in Jerusalem.

As a matter of fact, the Israeli society does not differ a great deal spiritually from *any* earthly society of today or any other day. Societies tend to have three major spiritual divisions—some kind of orthodox believers in something or other; some kind of middle-ground folk who are religious but not law-keeping; and finally, a majority of purely secular people who depend on whatever government is in power to take care of them. Back in Jesus' time the Jews were divided into three parties of different levels of reverence toward God—the Pharisees, the Sadducees, and the Herodians—and today there is not much difference.

The Pharisees were the meticulous Law-keepers, or apparent Law-keepers, who insisted on the proper performance of religious rite and ritual. They were the ones who checked out the Messiah's habits on the Sabbath, whether

His disciples washed their hands before they ate, and whether He would honor the Law by stoning the adulteress. They were the ones who wondered if His miracles came by virtue of the power of the devil. They sought to cross up the mind of Christ with questions and riddles in order to find some chink in the armor of the Messiah from Galilee. But they, too, in certain cases, were willing to grant the Lord at least a hearing, if not a sincere inquiry. Nicodemus was humble enough to seek a private audience with the youthful Teacher and to call Him "Rabbi." Joseph of Arimathea was wounded enough in spirit to sacrifice his own tomb at the death of the gentle Healer who had asked only for belief. Out of the scholarly Pharisees came Saul of Tarsus, whose brilliant teaching and keen perception of the will of God built the Church that overwhelmed the Roman Empire.

The Sadducees were not heard from as much in the Messiah's ministry. They were not likely to believe in miracles, and particularly not in the resurrection of the dead. They held to the Law and the Scriptures less stringently, perhaps, than the Pharisees, but they were barely looking for a Messiah. They greatly resembled today's Conservative Jews or liberal "Christians" in their basic adherence to some code based roughly on the existence of the Supreme Being, but they were not likely to bend over backward to please God. They tried, as so many people do (and always have done), to keep one foot firmly planted on realistic, secular ground while trying to put the other just inside the door of the house of worship. Their interest in Jesus was rather minimal, considering their religious preferences.

The Herodians were simply the secular people of the land who followed King Herod, or whomever, trying to live and let live in busy, dangerous, occupied Israel. They would not have known the Messiah if He stood before them, which in fact He did, and they had little interest in cultivating the remote Jehovah. They went to their jobs, conducted amicable enough relationships with the Romans, and looked for nothing special in life or death.

Looking at the groupings of the society of modern Israel, only the names have changed. Today Israel has the Orthodox Jews, who keep the Law, or at least the laws they have come to recognize as the Law; the "religious" Jews, who take pride in the land and their cultural heritage; and the clearly secular folk, who would feel just as much at home in New York City (and often do; New York City still contains more Jewish people than the land of Israel).

And Jesus gets just as little notice among the groups today as He did when He stood before them. Perhaps less, in fact, since it has become a basic tenet of at least Orthodox Judaism that belief in Jesus is anathema. Some Jewish scholars do examine Jesus for a variety of purposes, but only a handful acknowledge Him as their Messiah. For the others, He is dead and gone.

But Jesus *still does* live in Israel through the many and assorted Christians that are found throughout this singular nation. A good thing did indeed come out of Nazareth.

I traveled extensively through Israel seeking the Messiah, and I found Him being worshiped in various ways by sundry religious people. I found Him in strange churches, monasteries, and missions; I found Him on kibbutzim and in the fields. I was told He was at all of the vicious battles that periodically tear at that war-torn land, and in the front lines, as usual. I found His footprints on the Mount of Olives, in Nazareth, at the Wailing Wall, and on the surface of the Sea of Galilee. For those looking for Him, He is always there.

No matter how many people immigrate to Israel, the

groupings remain roughly the same, and the indifference to
Jesus among the Jewish citizens of the land remains pro-
portional. But the Gospel travels through Israel effectively
through visitors and tourists and an occasional witnessing
Christian whom God has called to live in this pioneer
nation. The Gospel is present and effective in the various
missions to the Israelites (Rom 10:1), and a precious few
learned, devout, old-Orthodox Jews tell their people the
truth that sets them free.

Naturally, among all those who immigrate are a few Jews
who at least recognize Jesus as an Israeli. Some Jewish
Christians enter the country, as do some Jews who are
"open" where the Messiah is concerned. Israel, as a nation
in the world, is as subject as any other nation to the tremendous outreach of the Gospel.

The policy called *Zionism* seeks to gather as many Jews
as will come to Israel. This is certainly scriptural: the
Jews have always belonged in their promised land. It is
scriptural for the future as well: the Messiah will return
to a Jewish Israel to initiate His Kingdom on earth. The
Jews who support Zionism are usually not really very cognizant of the scriptural validity of this good work, but just
the same, they will inexorably set up their part of God's
plan.

Zionism approaches Jews of every nation, color, and
creed, without regard for what sort of environment they
come from or what sort of philosophy they may hold.
Clearly, it is the opposite of racism, which it has been
called (in another setup of the ultimate plan for the end of
this present age).

Despite the overwhelming success of Zionist policies
since the restoration of Jewish Israel in 1948, the population of the Holy Land is slowly beginning to diminish. Jews
are starting to emigrate from Israel to other lands. A recent

American newsmagazine article, entitled "A Troubling Reverse Exodus," detailed the fact that some three hundred thousand Israeli Jews now live abroad, and this desertion of the promised land has been aggravated by a sudden 50 percent drop in immigration. "Jerusalem is just as alarmed by the fact that 40% of new immigrants from Western countries have returned to their original homelands within five years,"* the article specified.

Obviously there is a serious problem, and most Bible students would call it spiritual. It is one thing to undertake the pioneer life, to resettle a land, and to put one's sweat into sacred soil for the sake of one's God and one's beliefs. But it is quite another thing for *unspiritual* people to give up comforts merely for the sake of the fact that they are called Jewish. Naturally the vast majority of Israelis and immigrants are committed to the Israeli ideal—the true promised-land spirit—but there is an ever growing dissatisfied minority who judge their own lives not by God's promises but by the material benefits they can gain living in one place or the other.

It should be said, however, that throughout the past century there have been other "reverse exoduses," followed by a renewed immigration. Political times and seasons seem to be responsible.

If a person has Jewish parents but no God, he might as well have Gentile parents and no God; it makes little difference. Life is hard to the unbeliever and is estimated in terms of treasures stored here on earth. To the unspiritual Jew, neither biblically knowledgeable nor cognizant of God, Israel is merely a land of high taxes, inflation, and constant danger from all borders. No wonder he leaves, unaware of the heritage he spurns or the suffering of the past that made this land Jewish by God's will. One won-

*"A Troubling Reverse Exodus," *Time* 107(January 12, 1976):24.

ders how the saints of the original Exodus from Egypt must grieve over each emigrant who turns his back on the land of the prophets. The sacrificial Lamb, who still lives, must deplore this ungodly action.

But what else is to be expected when virtually every sign of God's presence, deeply connected to the Messiah in this Age of Grace, is absent? How should secular people act, except to seek a better secular life? Who can blame the exhausted Israeli unbeliever who has tilled the soil, fought the wars, lost the loved ones, and cast his lot with those who now appear to be international losers?

Jesus, of course, is the answer, and He will in fact save Israel when He returns (Rom 11:26).

But can He be found *today* in Israel?

In Israel, I personally attended two different Christian worship services. One was held at the Messianic Assembly of Jerusalem and the other at a homey little building known as the First Baptist Church of Jerusalem. The two churches atracted two different groups of Christians.

The building of the Messianic Assembly was something of a tourist attraction in its appeal to visitors from so many nations. I realized sadly that the Messiah, born a few miles south of the place, was brought there by strangers and worshiped by travelers. The service was clearly evangelical in nature, meant to appeal to the occasional unsaved Jew who happened by, rather like any American Board of Missions to the Jews service. There was no cross or baptistry in the place, and about all that marked it as distinctly Christian was the warm fellowship.

The little Assembly's meeting place was not well marked and, in fact, was hidden back in a yard, perhaps attesting to the cloak-and-dagger nature of Christian evangelism in Israel. It is not precisely illegal to witness for Christ in the Holy Land, but the government frowns on any sort of public demonstration. As it was explained to me, "My friend, we are trying to found a Jewish nation here on our own Jewish ground. We have nothing against a few Christians, but, after all, we have trouble enough taking care of our own." Except in individual, exceptional cases, there is no really violent reaction to the evangelism that does go on, and the Israelis, surrounded by churches of so many faiths, by Muslims, and even by adherents of Eastern religions, are a surprisingly tolerant lot.

Israel is dotted with Eastern Orthodox and Catholic churches, as well as settlements of exotic Christian-derived faiths from all over the world, and this tends to muddle, rather than make clear, the distinction between true Christian and Jew. Berobed black priests from Ethiopia carry the same crosses as American pastors and Russian monastics, and it is a little hard to blame the natives for thinking that all non-Jews come out of the same exotic mold.

As to the true belief in and appreciation of the Messiah to be found in all of these derivative religions, it probably varies with the individual. Some priests of strange denominations (strange, that is, to biblical Christianity) no doubt revere the Lord and serve Him in Israel because they consider that proper and fitting. Others probably have really little interest in the Lord per se but merely carry out the offices of their particular calling routinely and without regard to the particular setting. One priest was deported for gunrunning for the Palestinians!

The Messianic Assembly, then, comes somewhere in a long list of what the Israelis regard as the infinitely divided and inexplicable disciplines of Christianity. Tourists go there just as they go to the church in Bethlehem that is ostensibly built over the very spot of the manger. (At that church, the Israelis observe, priests of very specific splinter groups all but fight over the tourists—and their offerings—

even dividing the one building into various sectors! This
or that corner is said to be more holy than some other, and
visiting Christians are often disappointed by what has become of the Lord's humble beginnings.) The Assembly is
written off as a place where weary travelers can grab a
moment of the sort of worship they are used to, and who
can begrudge them that? (It should not be sold so short,
actually; the Assembly missionaries are skilled and dedicated men of the Gospel, and their small tree in Jerusalem
bears hearty fruit.)

The First Baptist Church, in all its humbleness, is a different matter altogether. This is very definitely a victorious, functioning, locally attended and supported, Bible-
teaching church. It has a membership of faithful Hebrew
Christian natives rather than an ever changing audience of
tourists, and it performs the functions of any Baptist
church. (It is by no means the only such church in Israel
or in Jerusalem, but it is the one I happened to attend and
can report on.)

That the unsaved Jews of Israel are as adverse to their
own Messiah as the Jews anywhere else is attested to by
the fact that they virtually never attend this church, though
they will occasionally stroll into the Messianic Assembly
building or similar places, strangely feeling more comfort-
able with Christian tourists than with Christians of their
own land. When you go to a church, you go to see Jesus,
they seem to feel; but when you go to a missionary organization, you go to exchange ideas, or whatever. The less
Jesus is involved, the better, their actions seem to say.
The Nazarene is best taken in small doses.

Of course, they may simply prefer the somewhat more
tactful approach of the average missionary as compared to
the straightforward praise of the Lord in the local churches.

There is a difference between witnessing and worship, though the churches also witness.

Missionaries are more likely to handle the Israeli people as the chosen people that they really are, in the manner and special respect that missionaries anywhere develop for the people whose language they have studied and whose salvation has become their prime ministry. The people of Israel, like people anywhere else, do occasionally have reasons to discuss God, and they expect that mission people will be somewhat more knowledgeable and respectful than confirmed churchgoers. They expect the missionaries to understand and sympathize with their special problem—that Jesus has become a virtual impossibility in Israel—and they expect to be listened to, even if only as debaters.

So the First Baptist Church of Jerusalem cannot boast of any great influx of unsaved Jews coming to seek the Messiah. But it does enjoy the faithful attendance of a healthy and happy group of Israeli Christians, who praise the Lord much as in the days of Christ's disciples. The fellowship is warm, the worship fulfilling, and the messages scholarly and accurate. The congregation prospers "even in Israel."

The night I attended the services at the First Baptist Church of Jerusalem, the place was filled to overflowing by an American tour group, primarily Gentile Christians. There was a guest speaker, an unsaved Israeli government official (I know of at least one saved Israeli government official). His message mostly concerned the politics of the time, shortly following the Yom Kippur War of 1973, since the largely American audience was to be thanked for the American support of Israel in that conflict. The official seemed to feel no special hesitancy about speaking in the church and was certainly aware of the many Israeli Christians who lined the pews. He did not touch upon religious matters, and in the question period he skillfully sidestepped questions about Tribulation-period prophecy ("The Russians? Well, I don't know. It's too risky to attempt prophecy in the land of the prophets!") The official certainly did not touch upon matters of spiritual gravity, such as the Messiah, and expected the courtesy to be returned. No one tried to corner him and witness, of course, because of the setting and his status as a guest; in any case, he was out of a back door two minutes after his talk was finished.

Israeli Christians, such as the members of that little church, do enjoy good fellowship among themselves, as we have said, but fellowship or even a courteous relationship with the rest of the nation is something else again. Many have been ostracized by their own families, in the old tradition; and when one lives in a nation so small and so special as Israel, it is especially saddening to be left out of things. The people of Israel would fit almost twice into Chicago, in terms of population, and so the whole nation is a family in a very real way. (This was especially telling in the Yom Kippur War, the government official pointed out: every family in Israel lost a relative.)

The Israeli Christians have to be loners or at least have to settle for each other's company primarily. They are marked people. There is little real action taken against them, but there is an unmistakable stigma where they are known. Yet, true to the example of their Lord, they carry their heavy cross publicly, with no attempts to hide their faith. They wear Christian crosses and fish symbols, carry New Testaments in the streets, and pray with their heads uncovered. They always proclaim Christ, regardless of vociferous opposition in some circles. They work on the kibbutzim, side by side with the unsaved Jews, and they invariably witness, getting stony reactions. The Lord must commend them.

One of the most exasperating ministries of every Israeli Christian is trying to impart the Bible, a wholly Israeli Book, to his countrymen. It is one thing to feel frustrated because one cannot persuade his neighbors to look into their own history; but it is quite another to be unable to even get their attention where real danger is concerned. End-times prophecy most certainly is gravely concerned with Israel, and the future of that land is inextricably bound up with God's plan for the end of this world as we know it.

Not everyone in Israel is ignorant of the Scriptures, of course, and there are even public competitions, almost like athletic meets, where learned scholars answer detailed questions about the Old Testament. This "Bible Bowl," as it were, shows at least an interest in the factual and biographical matter of Scripture. But in the all-important matters of irreverence, destiny, and the will of God, one would think the Bible were some kind of exotic, imported book of the occult. The average citizen in Israel knows little about it, except that somewhere within, it has a land grant for the territory and a statement about the Jews being chosen of God. It is doubtful if the average Israeli citizen, sometimes less biblically studied than even the American Jews, could locate those crucial precedents by chapter and verse.

This indifference to the Scriptures is simply the greatest and longest preserved failing of the chosen people. God was admonishing them for the same fault through Isaiah, Jeremiah, and a host of other prophets millennia ago, but the situation has hardly improved. It is utterly inexplicable that the world's most aged people, the monotheistic Jews, would now fail to honor their own God-inspired sages. Jesus lamented that a prophet was not without honor except in his own country, and truly His lament goes on.

Even if the Israeli people fail to look back in their history for useful precedents on how to conduct their nation under God today, one would think they would at least look ahead and see what the future holds. They are the ones who saw so many prophecies fulfilled; they are the ones who stand to gain or lose from actions concerning the future.

But they cannot even be convinced of so obvious and presently ominous a prophecy as the coming Russian invasion of Israel! Ezekiel placed this heinous act in the time after Israel's restoration and identified the parties concerned (Ezek 37-39), but either there is little recognition of Ezekiel in Israel today, or the expectation of a Russian invasion is not mentioned out of fear or discreet politics.

I interviewed one Israeli Christian, a political scientist, who approached the government officials and attempted to teach them about Ezekiel in modern terms. No one was impressed.

As it now appears, the entire Tribulation period will descend on Israel with the people utterly unaware, despite the clear and fearful prophecies available to all.

The Jews in general are not and never really were great appreciators of prophecy. They did not believe Jeremiah when he predicted the fall of the first Temple, nor Jesus concerning the fall of the second Temple. They did not believe the Torah in its explicit warnings of deportation and dispersion (Deut 28:64-66), and they have never believed the Messianic prophecies. They did not believe that Moses could intercede for them in the wilderness and get them food, and, in a general way today, they do not act as if they believe they are God's chosen people at all.

In fact, they act as if they are merely a competent, worldly nation of good fighters with good weapons, and they are getting their reward.

Before leaving the subject of the Jesus "blackout" in Israel, it should be mentioned that reconversion centers are at work in the Holy Land, so the Messiah's presence obviously has been noted. As with the American reconversion centers, the effort is made to reclaim Hebrew Christians for traditional Judaism, but with the difference that the atmosphere of Israel supposedly acts as a catalyst to the process. The reconversion candidates are given thorough tours of inspirational content, with the aim of persuading them that their homeland is worth more than some Gentile faith in a long-dead moralist.

But, as we have seen, Jesus' footprints are all over Israel, too, and why not? He was certainly the greatest Jew who ever climbed the Temple Mount, and His influence can be felt in the very air by Christians. Again, the reconversion rate is negligible, though American-Jewish families frequently send their Hebrew Christian children to the Holy Land for this extrapotent immersion into "real" Judaism. (Sometimes the reason for the pilgrimage is simply to get the youthful American away from Christian influence and into a "good Jewish environment," but the effort is frustrated by the plain fact that Israel, for all its relics and atmosphere, does not present a good, that is, biblically sound, Jewish environment.)

The general Israeli attitude toward Jesus is not to defame Him. He came and went, they think. He said some fine things—who can question His zeal for goodness, humility, self-sacrifice?—but this does not make Him the Messiah by any means. He was a great moral teacher, one of Israel's best, and He certainly ranks with at least the minor Jewish sages of history. But He led Jews astray, inspired an in-

valid Gentile worship of God, and left ignominiously via a
Roman cross. He is not expected back at all, and He is
written off as, at best, a false Messiah.

Where His teachings are concerned, there is little to
quibble with; today's Jews would not take a tough, Phari-
saical opposition to the Sermon on the Mount, for example.
But He is felt to have been inadequate for His time and
circumstances; He did and said much too little, considering
the great need. And, after all, He did *not* deliver His people from their endless troubles, as the Messiah is supposed
to do.

A certain amount of teaching, answering these typical
Jewish objections to Christ, goes on in the provinces on the
kibbutzim. It is not official teaching, of course, but Ameri-
can-Christian youngsters, and Christians of other nations,
find their way onto the farms and into the archaeological
diggings of Israel, where many extra hands are needed.
Guitar-strumming Christians sing the great Church hymns
by campfires, and they are accepted as folk music. The
words are heard and the messages felt, and time and again
young people are saved. They usually begin their Christian lives by keeping their new convictions a secret, but
the Lord sooner or later calls all His laborers into the fields,
and then they are exposed. They then pick up that peculiarly heavy cross and carry it among those "peculiar people"
God chose.

Someday, prophecy tells us, the Jews will all be regathered to the land of Israel. Someday the King will come and
reign in Jerusalem. Someday all the world will go up from
year to year to worship Him and to keep the Feast of Tabernacles, which will commemorate the establishment of
the Lord's tabernacle on the earth (Zech 14:16).

Until that day, the witness for Christ will go on in this
recalcitrant, courageous, beautiful land. Some will be

saved to leave and return, but most will be lost, the Jewish prophets lament. The Messianic Assembly, the First Baptist Church of Jerusalem, and all of the other true voices for salvation will continue to ring out in the promised land, uttering the final, most wondrous promise for all who can hear it:

The King is coming—and returning.
And to Israel, of all places!

7

Selling Refrigerators to Eskimos,
or
How to Witness to the Jews

Jewish people think they need Christ like the proverbial Eskimos need refrigerators. They have a perfectly adequate God, they say, and have no need of a magical man to intercede with Him on their behalf. They have no appetite for Gentile saviors, and they say they feel no real spiritual lack in their lives. They say they are the masters of monotheism, being much more experienced at it than any Christian or other sort of Gentile. They say, "Take it to your own people; we know them, and they need it."

Many Christians who witness vitally are still stymied when it comes to the Jews. Any missionary organization one can think of—Campus Crusade for Christ, Navigators, Gideons, Salvation Army, various denominational outreaches, to name a diverse few—is marked clearly by the absence of Jews in the ranks. More people have been sent the Gospel, with more prayers and at more expense and toil, in the jungles of the world than in the Jewish communities.

Yet the Messiah is Jewish. All of His disciples and all of His apostles were Jews. The Bible writers were all Jews. The first Christian church in the world, the mighty church

117

of Jerusalem, which sent the Gospel to the Gentile world, was almost wholly Jewish. The Father chose the Jews (Gen 12), the Son came to them exclusively (Matt 15:24), the Holy Spirit came to them on their feast of Pentecost (Acts 2). The Gospel is given "to the Jew first" (Rom 1:16).

We discussed earlier the rationale for witnessing to Jews. In this chapter, we hope to establish just how this marvel is accomplished.

We should first make clear the real Jewish objections to Christ, boiled down to their true meanings, without bias or tradition. The Jews have their reasons for rejecting Jesus, and the Christian witness who appreciates them will be that much closer to real communication with the chosen people. There are seemingly sound, bedrock reasons why Jesus will not do for the Jews, and Christians would do well to understand them.

The most biblically oriented basic objection to Jesus is the "plural covenant" reasoning of Jewish, and some Christian, theologians. God made two economies, says this theory, for basically different kinds of human beings: the Jews are chosen and saved by direct fiat of God, and the Gentiles are chosen and saved by virtue of the sacrifice of Jesus Christ. Those born Jewish come automatically into the promises to Abraham and automatically (that is, without a savior) are saved. The Gentiles, heathens to whom God gave no law, must individually accept Christ's redemptive work to qualify for salvation. There are simply two different covenants for two separate peoples, says this reasoning.

One might immediately claim John 14:6, "No man cometh unto the Father, but by me," in which Jesus certainly seemed to be addressing the human race as a whole. But here the advocate of the plural covenant says, "This doesn't apply to people who do not have to come to the Father, because they are already with Him." The Jews, having been chosen, do not need to be chosen again. This kind of thinking might read: "No man need come unto the Father who is with Him already."

While the Jewish man on the street may not comprehend or be able to state this philosophy, he does act it out in his mannerisms when the evangelist comes (if he ever comes). The Jew acts an almost superior role in godly things, resting in his chosen status and assuming that Christ is "for the *goyim.*" His rabbi has indicated this clearly, his longevity in world history seems to bear it out, and his morally and materially successful community of fellow Jews seems the final proof. Jews must indeed be God's favorites, despite Gentile jealousy and persecution, and they certainly need no special savior in order to come to their very own Father.

The answer to this objection—that it does violence to the Gospel—is no answer to the Jew. He says, "The Gospel, whatever that is, is *your* book, not mine." In truth, the Gospel looks absurd if the plural covenant is accurate; Jesus wasted His entire ministry witnessing only "unto the lost sheep of the house of Israel," (Matt 15:24) people already saved, according to this position. Paul's appeal, "Brethren, my heart's desire and prayer to God for Israel is, that they might be saved" (Rom 10:1), seems a useless exercise if Israel is already saved, and the Pharisee-Christian Paul, so studied in the Old Testament, seems to have missed its point entirely.

But again, the Jew does not regard the New Testament as God's Word. He must be shown, if he is willing to look, that the idea of a special covenant for Jews only, outside of Christ, is irreconcilable with the *Old* Testament. The Jew must be made to understand that God did not choose the Jews for salvation but, rather, to bring salvation to the world as well as to themselves (John 4:22).

Obviously, much of the prophecy of the Old Testament concerning the Messiah has to be discarded if the Jews are already saved without a Messiah. That involves excising or reinterpreting over three hundred prophecies that refer to Jesus' first advent alone (some Jewish scholars, especially at the reconversion centers, are already at the task of reinterpreting all of the Messianic prophecies, and they come up with ingenious, if superficial, evasions).

Then, the entire idea of sacrifice for redemption, the outstanding feature of biblical Judaism, must be discarded. After all, if every Jew born today is saved and no Jew is doing his sacrifices today (there being no Temple of God in Jerusalem), then redemption *does not* require sacrifice. Or we have the untenable proposition that at the whim of the Gentiles, the Jewish Temple was thrown down, not once but twice in history; and God's plans for His chosen people had to be changed, changed back, and changed still again. If the Jew today is saved just because he is Jewish, he is certainly enjoying a more lenient economy than his ancestors ever did, and God has grown lax in His commandments. (Actually, of course, the sacrifices pointed to the Messiah's ultimate sacrifice, which saves Israel and all other nations.)

The plural covenant also fails against an accurate reading of the Law of the Torah, with its many conditional clauses and its threats of the removal of chosen-person status from violators. Deuteronomy 28 serves to show that every Jew is by no means saved just because he is born of Jews; he has much to do to honor this heritage, and it is possible for him to fail (and the unfortunate prophecy of verses 64-66 has been terrifyingly realized for world Jewry in their almost universal failure). The harsh law concerning the Day of Atonement carried the penalty of the Jew being "cut off from among his people" for a minor violation (Lev 23:29).

Jewish salvation could certainly and most easily be lost in view of the difficulty of accurately performing Old Testament Judaism. None of us would want to depend on fulfilling the infinitely complex prescriptions of Jehovah without the intercession of His Son, and none of us have to.

The Christian theologians who embrace the plural covenant are generally looking for an easy answer to a hard problem. However convenient it might be to consider that the Jews are already taken care of by God, or however relaxing it may be to community relations, the Jews still need salvation, each one individually, as with all other men.

Any Hebrew Christian can attest to the profound difference between the nominal satisfaction he once felt as a chosen person of the Jewish community and the miraculous life he has today in Christ. Judaism is simply not able to be truly appreciated by the unsaved Jew.

Apart from the plural covenant, which attempts to place the Jew in some kind of special spiritual class, most other objections rest on understandable worldly grounds.

Mal Couch, a distinguished Christian film maker and the president of Evangelical Communications Research Foundation, has made it his lifework to witness to the chosen people and cultivate the powers that be in Israel. He has witnessed to many Jews, has read extensively in the rabbinical commentaries, and has achieved the ultimate compliment as a missionary to the chosen people: he was accused of being Jewish in a letter to the editor of *Moody Monthly*.

He has compiled a list of the top thirteen Jewish reasons for objecting to Christ and His Church. They are roughly in order of importance, as presented below, but this would vary from Jew to Jew, depending on life experiences (we *are* dealing with a people who live everywhere and have seen just about everything). It is well for the Christian witnessing to Jews to understand these objections thoroughly and, perhaps, to appreciate the validity of some of them. The Jew is not merely stubborn; he thinks hard, and he has come to some of his conclusions through very bitter experience and long meditation.

1. *The persecution of the Jews in the name of Christ.* We do not need to rehearse it again, but there is much to make up for in the black days when professing Christians massacred the chosen people.

2. *The Nazi holocaust.* This unmitigated horror, unprecedented in man's history, bludgeoned out of the minds of many Jews any thought of a spiritual life and any hope for a better world. The idea of genocide against one's own people promotes a bitterness that precludes the message of the Gospel in all its hope. Many of the older generations of Jews simply wish to be left alone to see if they can die in their beds.

3. *The Talmud and the other rabbinical commentaries, which tie the Jewish faith tightly to traditional laws.* As long as these old books, written by men and sometimes disagreeing with the Scripture itself, define Judaism, salvation based on grace—the free gift of God—is meaningless to the Jew. If the Jew thinks that the separation of milk and meat dishes is important to God, he obviously has some trouble seeing that God is willing to no longer remember his serious sins. As long as the Talmud prescribes a legal framework as pleasing to God, forgiveness based on a long-gone Savior is unthinkable. The Talmud is generally held in more esteem by modern rabbis, at least judging by their actions, than the Torah itself.

4. *Nineteen centuries without a sacrificial system.* With-

out sacrifices to look upon as acceptable to God, the Jew has forgotten the price of redemption and substituted his own good works system. The book of Hebrews was addressed to Jews who could *see* their high priest perform in the Temple and who counted on gaining their redemption, however temporary, through the sacrifices he made. To them, Jesus was at least a logical extension of Judaism as they understood it, if not the very fulfillment of it. Today the Jews do not see genuine Judaism performed; thus, they fail to appreciate the beauty of God's plan for redemption by sacrifice. Nineteen centuries is a long time; there is an entirely new Jew today, and he acts as if God has changed the Jewish religion to accommodate him.

5. *The line of false Messiahs.* A number of illustrious, and not so illustrious, men have claimed to be the Messiah throughout Jewish history, and those Jews who followed these frauds were shunned and laughed at. Those who followed Bar Kochba (135 B.C.) were annihilated by Hadrian and the Roman legions after their "invincible" leader was felled in a minor skirmish. Those memories are bitter. Worse even than failing to wait hopefully for the real Messiah in Judaism is going after a false one. There are many questions about Jesus—Why did He not bring His Kingdom of heaven that was "at hand"? Why did He not defeat the Romans and rule the world? How could He be taken in the midst of His ministry and crucified? As long as any Messiah remains open to question, the Jews are not eager to place their faith in him.

6. *The name Jesus Christ.* "Jesus Christ is Greek to me," the Jew might well say, and he is absolutely right. The name we have given in English to *Yeshua Hamashiah* ("Joshua, the Messiah") is a turnoff to the Jews. They do not recognize *Jesus Christ* as a Jewish name, and of course it isn't. It isn't even an English translation of a Jew-

ish name. It is a transliteration of a Greek name. This is
not even understood by many Christian leaders, but the
Messiah's name was written in Greek in the original Greek-
language gospels that we have. The King James Bible
translators rendered that Greek equivalent into English
letters so that it could be pronounced relatively the same
way as it sounded in the original Greek. This is quite reasonable and does not represent any mischief on the part of
the translators. Translators normally transliterate proper
names rather than translating them. We did not change
Solzhenitsyn to Solomon or Smith when we translated his
books into English, but we rendered the Russian lettering
into English lettering as nearly as we could. Mischief on
the part of the King James translators can be found in Acts
12:4, where "Easter" is purposely substituted for "Passover," which appears in the original. Most church congregations cannot answer the question, "What is Jesus'
name in English?" The answer is *Joshua*, the direct translation of *Yeshua;* and when we realize that, we see a beautiful biblical symbol, because Joshua was the one God used
to take His people to their promised land at the sound of
the trumpet, as will his antitype, Joshua of Nazareth. This
is not such an important matter to Christian believers, but
to the Jews it becomes all-important. I often wonder how
many more Jews would come easily to a Messiah whose
name, *Joshua*, fit right into the Jewish community. It is
eye-opening to meditate on the fact that no one in Israel
would ever have called the Carpenter of Nazareth *Jesus*.

7. *The Meshummed complex*. A *Meshummed* is a traitor.
The supposed repudiation of one's own people, which is
involved when a Jew accepts the Messiah, has effectively
kept Jews away from Him by the millions. One does wonder how many Jews are "closet" believers, however, un-

willing to face the persecution they would receive as Jewish Christians in their communities.

8. *The mistaken focus on the Old Testament as a book of law.* The Old Testament certainly presents a great deal of law, but its point is *faith*. Abraham was not the friend of God because he obeyed so well. Actually, he displeased God a great deal, and his personal sins are unimaginably grave by today's Jewish or Christian standards. But God counted Abraham's faith as righteousness. He stumbled and fell, but he *believed*. This man, who twice sold off his wife as his sister and gladly collected the spoils, ultimately offered God his only son in sacrifice. Later on, God Himself went through with that same sacrifice in order to save the world. David and his son Solomon, the builder of the mighty first Temple of God, had terrible violations of the Law in their lives; but they were *believers* in God, and their *faith* was acceptable to Him. While the sacrifices, done so routinely, stank in God's nostrils, He still was able to count for the disgusted Elijah seven thousand who had not bowed the knee to Baal (1 Kings 19:18). God values, and has always valued, *faith* above mere Law-keeping. Today's Jew regards the Old Testament as a lawbook, but in fact does not keep its laws, or even make a serious attempt to. Faith hardly enters the Jewish picture, being rather taken for granted, though its absence is conspicuous to a true believer.

9. *Liberalism—the modern Jewish culture.* We have discussed at length the function of tradition and the Jewish community "mystique." Its function in keeping the Jews away from so original an idea as the Messiah having already come is manifest.

10. *Jealousy of the Gentiles.* It is hard to say, for a Hebrew Christian, whether the Jews are more jealous of the

Gentiles than the Gentiles are of the Jews. The secret admiration both societies hold for each other in times of friendship or fighting is quite apparent to those with relationships in both communities. But, in any case, God Himself once said that He would provoke the chosen Jews to jealousy of the ordinary Gentile believers, and so He has. "I will move them to jealousy with those which are not a people," God vowed (Deut 32:21*b*) in answer to His children causing Him (God!) to become jealous (v. 21*a*). The Gentiles (not the Jews) control the business world, the banks, the military, and the governments everywhere, and the Jews, confident that they could do as well, given the chance, do get jealous. Paul directed Christian attention to this jealousy as it applied to the recognition of Christ (Rom 10:19), and there the jealousy festers. The Jews do not really know what to make of a truly victorious Christian Gentile. That is not supposed to happen (unless the particular Jew holds to the plural covenant, which admits to Gentile salvation). Many times I can feel the jealousy of a fellow Jew burning right through me as my brother perceives the peace I have in Christ. He is jealous of a saved Gentile, too.

11. *Lack of spiritual grasp.* By and large, the Jews today have no appreciation of the supernatural quality of religious life. Their legal system is bound to certain performances and the flexibility to allow for human failings, and thus they never see a miracle. They "being ignorant of God's righteousness, and going about to establish their own righteousness" (Rom 10:3) miss the point of God's plan for them. Paul said plainly, "I bear them record [and Paul was Jewish, of course] that they have a zeal for God, but not according to knowledge" (v. 2). The Jewish zeal for God is usually apparent, but, as the apostle states, it is not

really based on any knowledge of who God is. It is more an affectation than a sound faith based on Scripture, in which God is flawlessly explained. It is, in fact, a kind of "Jewish chauvinism" to praise God—an act that makes one very Jewish indeed—while God remains remote and virtually unknowable in the Jewish mind.

12. *Failure to perceive the Jewish obligation to receive the Messiah.* "Who hath believed our report?" Isaiah cries at the outset of his stunningly appropriate chapter about Jesus and His ministry (Isa 53). It is a tragic chapter explaining that the Messiah goes "as a lamb to the slaughter" but goes unrecognized by His own. This is the very point that the Hebrew Christian, or Messianic Jew, harps on—that the unsaved Jews have missed the central core of Judaism and are thus not adequate Jews at all in God's eyes. There is a Jewish *obligation* to receive the Messiah. All of the sacrifices of the Old Testament—each man's individual, arduous sacrifices—are utterly without redeeming value if the Messiah goes unaccepted. God went along with an unregenerate people for nearly two thousand years, looking toward the Messiah's retroactive acceptance of the sacrifices and culmination of them in the new covenant (Rom 3:25). If the Messiah passes unaccepted, the new covenant simply does not go into force for the chosen people, and they languish without hope. As it stands now, without a Temple for sacrifices, the individual Jew is unable to practice the old covenant, and he has left himself outside of the new covenant as well. Scripturally, it is difficult to see how he has any more hope than any heathen on the earth.

13. *Failure to recognize that the old covenant ended.* Jeremiah 31:31-34, which we reviewed in chapter 1, has been totally missed by the modern Jew. He has not seemed to realize that the Law had an ending point, a fulfillment.

He goes on as if a legal system will please God, even though God stated plainly that a new covenant was to go into effect with the Messiah. It should be obvious that the days of the Old Testament are gone in more ways than one. Men do not converse with God now; Temple sacrifices cannot be offered now; prophets in the streets no longer foreshadow the coming of the Messiah; no high priest ever goes before God with the nation's sins on the Day of Atonement anymore. Yet the Jews act as if the Old Testament and the various commentaries are still contemporary religion, pleasing to God. They should surely spot that there is simply a different kind of spiritual economy going on now. The behavior of Christians—primarily Gentiles who worship the true God—certainly presents a different picture from the old one of the non-Jewish nations. But the old covenant, crippled by inexplicable traditions and modified by endless generations of well-meaning sages and rabbis, remains the Jew's only claim to scriptural validity. It ended nearly two thousand years ago and has no further validity, but it still remains the shaky keystone of modern Judaism.

Those are Mr. Couch's "top thirteen" Jewish objections to Jesus. Listed one by one, they seem to present a formidable obstacle to the sharing of the Gospel, and they truly put the Jews in a class by themselves as people who do not want the Messiah. Every one of the objections, except the lack of spiritual grasp, which is seen in all sectors of today's society, is peculiarly Jewish and peculiarly difficult to deal with.

How shall we, after all, make excuses for Jewish persecution? It happened. They felt it deeply, and they have good memories. As we have seen, they are still afraid of such a thing as the holocaust in some new incarnation. How shall we combat the tenacity of the Law, the accusation of "traitor" upon the heads of those who come to the Messiah, and the pervasive "liberal" religion of the synagogues?

I am often asked the simple question, "How do you witness to the Jews?" It actually does have a simple answer, or at least an answer that can be simply stated. There are only two elements that I have found to be effective in sharing the faith with Jews, and every Christian has both in good supply. They may be hard to put into use, but if these two elements are brought to the Jew so that he can really feel them and see them, he can easily come to His Messiah. The two elements are:

1. Love
2. The Bible

It seems all too simple.

And, as a matter of fact, the same two elements would apply to witnessing to Gentiles as well. Anyone who can feel love and who can realize the significance of the Bible as God's Word will be open to receiving Christ.

Let us deal with these two elements. The reason more Jews do not come to Christ is that the love they feel from Christians is insufficient to interest them in the Christian faith. And the reason more Jews do not come to Christ is that they do not understand that the Bible is God's Word.

Let's face it. The love that Jews feel from Christians is not even enough for the Jews to feel secure living among them. It is not even enough for the Jews to be able to distinguish Christians from unsaved Gentiles. It is not even enough to keep the Jews from being downright *afraid* of their Christian neighbors!

Jews tend to describe Gentiles, Christian and otherwise, as cool, remote, reserved people with the capacity for unpredictable viciousness. They well remember the modicum of Christian help that was available in the time of

Hitler; it wasn't sufficient to get the Church a passing grade. They still regard a smiling Christian as a Greek bearing gifts. They are well aware of the established Christian church members who study the Scriptures on Sunday morning and learn that the Jews are God's chosen people, and then go out in the afternoon to play golf at a country club where no Jews are admitted.

Love for the Jew has to overcome all of that, but, believe me, it is absolutely necessary to the witness for Christ. No wonder they don't recognize Christians among the Gentiles; didn't their own Messiah say His disciples would be known by their love? Don't we in the Church sing, "And they'll know we are Christians by our love"?

Well, they don't know we are Christians.

I am aware that the Jews make themselves a bit difficult to love. They have an "in-group," and we have already discussed the many reasons for this. It is hard to break into that inner circle when trust is dispensed. But everybody needs love. Everybody's children need love, and the Jews are God's children. And we all know that children who have been hurt need *more* love than others.

This is a matter for prayer for most Gentile Christians. I come by my love for my people honestly; I grew up with them, and I think they are terrific. But Christian Gentiles need to pray for love for the Jews. God will surely grant this prayer; He has plenty of love for the Jews Himself, and He has said that we are to be like Him. Jesus' hard command, "Be ye therefore perfect, even as your Father which is in heaven is perfect" (Matt 5:48) is never harder than when we apply it to loving those whom God loves, whether they be thieves, adulteresses, lepers, or Jews.

Of course, we come by a wonderful blessing from God when we accomplish this particular command ("I will bless them that bless thee"—the Jewish nation, see Gen 12:3*a*).

And we avoid a curse from the lips of the Father Himself, which many have suffered in the past ("And I will . . . curse him that curseth thee," v, 3*b*),

Love for the Jew does not mean worship of him. Christians do not worship men. When Peter, the most distinguished Jewish Christian of the moment, approached Cornelius, the Roman "fell down at his feet, and worshipped him. But Peter took him up, saying, "Stand up; I myself also am a man" (Acts 10:25-26). It was an excellent demonstration of new-covenant thinking: men are equal sinners, and only God is good. Thus, we do not revere the Jewish people. (But the Gospel is to go "to the Jew first," as Paul states [Rom 1:16], prays [Rom 10:1], and finally insists [Rom 11:1].)

Loving the Jew, then, does not consist of some kind of reverence: the Jew would consider that foolish on the part of Christians. It *does* consist of recognizing that the Jew is a human being with hopes and dreams and aches and pains, like all other men; it consists of recognizing that the Jew is away from home everywhere but in Israel and therefore is invariably in need of the normal courtesies we extend to at least out-of-town visitors; it consists of abhorring every sort of anti-Semitism, from United Nations pronouncements against Zionism to those local country clubs; it consists of laying off the stereotyping of Jews that insults them (they are not all tailors, moneylenders, and rich doctors), and it consists today of supporting the State of Israel, a profoundly Christian thing to do.

We might boil it all down to a brilliant statement by "an ancient Rabbi": "Love thy neighbour as thyself" (Matt 19:19).

It is not enough to just repeat that profound, godly lesson in human relations. We must meditate on it and practice it. We must picture what it would be like if the Jew

were in power and had treated Christians in the way he has
been treated. If part of *your* family were missing, as part
of every Jewish family is today, because the Nazis put them
in gas chambers, how much love would you need to make
up for it? Can you spare that much?

In treating Jews as we ourselves would like to be treated,
it is well to remember that in their extremely long history
the Jews, who were many times in real positions of power,
persecuted no one. They fought when there was fighting to
be done, but what have they done to be so universally de-
spised? When have they dealt out to their neighbors what
they themselves have absorbed? Don't they deserve better
treatment? Even genuine love?

Love is the electric circuit that makes the Gospel travel
and do work. If you will "wire in" a Jew, you will find that
he is a good conductor. The person who first witnessed to
me (and I came to Christ as a result of that one witness)
loved me. She is very happy now, as Mrs. Levitt, and she
has seen the one Jew she spoke up to reach out in books,
films, radio, and teaching to literally millions. I don't mind
telling you that my witness and ministry are powerful, in
the grace of God, and it is in large part because I am Jewish.

Love a Jew. When he comes to the Messiah, stand back
amazed and watch what your one little love can do!

We need so many more Jews in the Church, God knows.
We need them to make the Jewish Scriptures clear, if for
nothing else. I amaze Gentile Christians every Sunday
with common information, known to almost any Jew, having to do with the nature of God and His Word. We Jews
have been thinking about these things for some time now,
and, guided in the right direction, we have plenty to say.
If you did not sit down to Passover annually for thirty-two
years as I did, then I naturally have a thing or two to impart to you about what it really means. If you have not

practiced kissing each page of Scripture as you open it, then the aged Jewish scholars have something to tell you about respect for God and His Word. (And you, of course, have things to tell them. God wants us *together*—"One in Christ"—in the Church, Eph 2:14).

Enough of love. You have it in good measure, and you have Christ, a dependable source for it if you should need a little extra when confronting your Jewish friend. Godspeed.

My second element in witnessing to Jews was simply the Bible. By that I mean that we must somehow bring the Jew back to his own Book, written by his own writers, inspired by his own God. It seems strange, of course, to have to make a special effort to make a great chef see that his best dish tastes wonderful, but we have seen that the Jew has come away from the Bible in his long time of tradition-making. Astoundingly, even the aged Jews who kiss each page of Scripture as they study it do not really believe it to be the infallible Word of God. They are giving it the respect we give the American flag when we kiss it, and we properly do not regard the flag as a work of God.

We saw above what has happened in the way of tradition, the introduction of the works of sages and rabbis, and the institution of new laws to enhance the Jewish legal system. All of these contribute to the Jewish misunderstanding of the role of the Bible in Judaism. It will be hard for the Jew of today to believe, but he must be told in plain terms that the Bible is the only valid, godly Book about Judaism.

I have read the Talmud. I have read it in Hebrew and discussed it with learned men. I am by no means an expert on it, but I have performed the traditional exercises of interpreting its law through lengthy discussion and applying its principles to practical matters. Some of it is very beau-

tiful ("Never make a woman cry; God counts her tears"),
and some of it is painfully picky when it comes to legal issues. But until I read the Bible, I had not read God's Word,
and that was very clear to me. A successful life, pleasing to
God, is fully explained in the Bible; no further commentary
is necessary, as Christians have shown. Salvation is explained in full in the Bible also; it is not based on the merits
or good works of men (Eph 2:8-9).

In the letters in chapter 2 we saw how casually many
Jewish people referred to the Bible, saying we do not have
to believe "every word" of it; it would be useless without
the commentaries, and so forth. This is the attitude that
must be corrected if the Jew is to find his way to the Messiah. The way to the Messiah is explained in the Bible and
in the Bible alone; it is not effectively shown by Christians;
it is not convincingly imparted in four or five or however
many spiritual laws; and it is not sincerely told by preachers in most church pulpits. At least not to most Jews. Naturally some Jews are saved by a good Christian witness, by
little booklets of laws, and by skillful preachers of the Gospel.

But those methods do not compare with the idea of the
Jew *finding his own Messiah in his own Book.* If the Jews
find out that the whole Bible is God's love letter to men,
there will not have to be any more books like this one.
The whole sandstone house of traditional Judaism—designed to lead men to God, but ironically keeping them
away from Him—will fall down when the Jew reads his
own Scripture. And the Jew will know how to build a new
house on rock.

So, how do you get a Jew to read his Book? Well, remember that this is step two; first you have to love him.

But assuming that you and some Jewish person do have
a loving relationship, it is then only necessary to demon-

strate to him that *you* value the Scriptures and find them true and accurate. You can demonstrate the conditions of the dispersion from the Scriptures (Deut 28), the character of the Messiah at His first advent (Isa 53), the clear fact that the Messiah was to come before the second Temple was destroyed (Dan 9:25-26), the resettling of Israel by the Jews (Ezek 37), and a host of other plain, provable facts found in Scripture. If these prophecies were fulfilled, then what about the Messianic Scriptures? There are hundreds. Challenge your friend to find prophecies about the Messiah that Jesus did not fulfill, or will not fulfill in the context of His prophesied second coming. Visit a mission to the Jews and get a complete copy of Messianic Scriptures and their fulfillments in Christ.

If all of this makes you do some extra Bible study, it has never been known to be harmful. By studying the problem of how to witness to the Jewish people, I, for one, have found myself having to read the whole Bible and understand a lot of theology. In my experience, it is the most pleasant, blessed work on earth, and our Father certainly smiles on it.

And that is all I can say on witnessing to the Jews. As a Jewish Christian, I know it is not all that difficult; it just has to be tried. I have listed the host of Jewish objections to Jesus from several sources so that you will be ready for them. And I have given two suggestions that, if carried out in full, I feel certain will result in the salvation of many Jews.

I should say just one more thing about this difficult ministry: do not get discouraged. God well knows that witnessing to the Jews is difficult; He was watching carefully when it was tried by the best Witness. You are not going to bring every Jew to Christ any more than you could expect to bring every Gentile to Christ. Don't be tempted to think, "Well, God was right; they *are* stiff-necked." We have already discussed why you might find a little stiffness among Jewish necks.

But if you love these people and show them your Bible, some will definitely respond. It has been tried, and it works. And you will be blessed for it.

Talk to your Jewish friends. Ask one of them how to pronounce the word *l'chaim.*

L'chaim means "To life!" and that's a great place to start!

8

For a Limited Time Only

Today's scholars of prophecy feel that the Jews, and everybody else among the unbelievers, had better make up their minds about Christ immediately. It is possible that the free gift of salvation is now available "for a limited time only."

Of course Christians have been warning of the end of the world for quite some time now. The apostles expected an early rapture of the Church, even within their lifetimes. The "day and hour" have always been God's secret, as the Scripture says clearly (Matt 24:36), but it is possible for students of prophecy to arrive at an approximate timing of the end by carefully comparing world affairs and prophetic Scripture.

It should be said plainly, in advance of any such speculations about the "end times," that such calculations are done in a spirit of questing; no one has any sort of absolute information on this.

But believers are admonished to be steadily ready for the end (1 Thess 5:1-6), and it is far better that we continue to anticipate an early coming, as the New Testament writers did, than to be caught unawares. A Christian has no reason to be surprised by the coming of the Lord for His Church, and believers should take note of those events in the world that could indicate the period of tribulation that is to follow the rapture.

Many fine books on prophecy discuss in full the various events to be expected in connection with the biblical end times. It is beyond our scope here to go into complete definitions, but a schedule of these events should be considered now in the light of the Jewish future as well as the future (or lack of it) of the rest of the world. The Jews will be in a unique position, as usual, when the end times come upon the world. And, unfortunately, strife-torn Israel is to be the focal point of the worst devastation of the period.

There is much discussion about what event comes first in the prophetic picture of the end times. Some scholars expect the rapture of the Church—the moment when Christ comes to meet the believers in the air (1 Thess 4:16-17)— to begin the final series of events, and others hold that the rapture comes later, after the seven-year Tribulation period or at its midpoint. I personally expect the rapture to come first, and with each book I write I wonder whether it will reach a Christian public or a readership totally absent of Christians (who will have already gone with the Lord in the rapture). In my view, the rapture could come before you finish reading this sentence, and that is the way the Lord characterized this particular event ("in the twinkling of an eye," 1 Cor 15:52; "as a thief in the night," 1 Thess 5:2). I have not been able to see the validity of the other positions, because they preclude a "surprise" rapture; anyone could schedule the rapture on their calendar, if it is to be expected at the midpoint or the end of the Tribulation period, and be packed and ready to go. Also, it is not consistent with the biblical promises to believers that they should remain on earth for the tragedies of the Tribulation period, "for God hath not appointed us to wrath, but to obtain salvation by our Lord Jesus Christ" (1 Thess 5:9).

In any case, the beginning of the Tribulation period will be a clearly marked event: the signing of a seven-year covenant, or treaty, between the Antichrist, the coming world ruler, and Israel (Dan 9:27; in Daniel's parlance, one week equals seven years). This covenant is usually construed as a false promise by the Antichrist to guarantee Israel's security, rather in the spirit of so many other false treaties we have seen in this century (e.g., Hitler, Stalin).

This treaty may well result from an abortive Russian invasion of Israel (Ezek 38-39), which will cause Israel to start looking for a sound offer of peace backed by might. The Russian invasion is another event connected to the end times that has proved difficult to place on a "schedule." It will be over in a day, perhaps, or at least it will be a very brief encounter, as pictured by Ezekiel, and I view it as happening early in the seven-year period or just prior to it (but after the rapture of the Church).

For the first half of his contracted period, the Antichrist will maintain the peace, but his steady rise in power to a globally dominant position apparently will go to his head. At the midpoint of the Tribulation period, he will enter the Temple of God in Jerusalem (to be rebuilt) and declare himself God! (Dan 9:27; Matt 24:15; 2 Thess 2:3-4). This one-of-a-kind blasphemy will begin the Great Tribulation, as the Lord called it: "For then shall be great tribulation, such as was not since the beginning of the world to this time, no, nor ever shall be. And except those days should be shortened, there should no flesh be saved" (Matt 24: 21).

From there the world situation seems to deteriorate into a final war, the likes of which will make all previous wars fade into mild disagreements. The surviving might of the world will gather in the quiet, level plain in Israel called Armageddon, where enormous armies will fight until the Lord comes to put a final end to the butchery, lest "no flesh be saved."

The believers will return with the Lord, and after a brief judgment separating out the Christians who came to faith during the Tribulation period (Matt 25:31-46), the Kingdom will be gotten under way on earth. All surviving Israel will be saved (Rom 11:26), and believers of all periods—Old Testament, Church age, and Tribulation—will at last reign in the world in peace. God's will shall be done on earth as it is in heaven.

This Kingdom, or Millennium, as it is sometimes called, will last one thousand years. The King will then hold a final judgment. On this so-called Judgment Day, He will relegate all unbelievers to the "lake of fire" and all believers to endless bliss in the presence of God.

It can be seen from the foregoing schedule of events that the Jew is in a unique position in regard to the end times. If he is saved now, before the rapture, he will become a member of the Church and go with the Lord when He comes. If he is saved during the Tribulation period, he will go into the Kingdom, but without the advantages of the seven years in heaven with Christ, the avoidance of the Tribulation disasters, and the metamorphosis of his body (1 Cor 15:51-52). He will enter the Kingdom as a natural man in that case, although death will have been abolished for believers, and he will survive the thousand years and enter eternity. But, finally, and unfortunately, this will be the case for most Jews: if he is not saved now and not saved during the Tribulation period, he will be obliged to survive until Armageddon to gain his salvation. "All Israel shall be saved" when the Lord returns after the Tribulation period (Rom 11:26; Zech 12:9–13:1), but the Scripture refers to all *living* Israel.

It will be very hard for any given Jewish person to make it all the way to Armageddon. "And it shall come to pass, that in all the land, saith the LORD, two parts therein shall be cut off and die," warns Zechariah. "And I will bring the third part through the fire,   and they shall say, The Lord is my God" (Zech 13:8-9). Only one-third of Israel will live to see the return of the King.

It is sad that a mere third of the people once chosen for glory will live to see it. But, in plain words, the Jew today has the choice of (1) coming to the Messiah now, (2) coming to Him under terrible duress in the Tribulation period, or (3) trying against bad odds to be among the surviving one-third of Israel at Armageddon.

Sadder still is the fact that the Jew is all but unaware of this prophetic dilemma, though we have quoted the Old Testament liberally in explaining it. It is *his* treaty that will be broken, *his* Temple that will be desecrated, *his* land that will be torn apart with terrible war. It was *his* prophets that specified all of this, and *his* Gospel that provides the way out of it.

The unsaved Gentile has, of course, even worse prospects than the Jew. He does not have a ghost of a chance at Armageddon; and if he is not saved before then, he has no chance of salvation at all. At least a portion of Israel will be saved, honoring God's promise to His friend Abraham that his nation would endure forever. But the unsaved Gentile is doomed at the climax of the Tribulation period. It goes without saying that a continuing witness to the Gentiles is mandatory, but that is another book.

I collect news clippings of current events that seem to point to an early Tribulation period. This has become a hobby with me, as I am often asked to speak on prophecy, especially to justify my own position that the end times are very near. I watch the newspapers and magazines for news around the world that suggests that the days of the Antichrist are in preparation. I compare my list of news events with Matthew 24, that electrifying and de-

tailed answer to the disciples' question, "Tell us, when shall
these things be? And what shall be the sign of thy coming, and of the end of the world?" (24:3). I look at the
words of the prophets, and especially at the book of Revelation, for the developing conditions of the Tribulation
times.

And I have collected quite a list of items that seem to
justify being ready at this time for the rapture and the
Tribulation period. Many of the phenomena of world eco-
nomics and politics have not been seen before; that is, this
generation is special in prophecy fulfillment. Many of the
news events I have collected were never seen by past generations; and though Christians have rightly warned the
world all through the Church age to be in readiness for the
end, never before have they had so good an argument for
that position.

Finally, most of my list of events concerns the presence
of an agonized Israel, resettled by Jews, a prerequisite of
end-times prophecy. Unfortunately, most of the dire proceedings given below pertain to the already beleaguered
State of Israel, as we would expect in connection with the
end of God's plan for the earth.

To begin with, we are possibly seeing the Russian invasion of Israel being set up now. It used to take quite a
bit of argument, back before the resettlement of the promised land and before Russia became a real power, to justify
Ezekiel's clear-eyed forecast of this end-times event (Ezek
38-39). But today we are observing a Russian expansion
in the Middle East in general, and a steadily increasing
Russian animosity toward Israel in particular. This prophecy did not quite fit with Ezekiel's analysis until the au-
tumn of 1975, when Egypt and Russia had a falling out;
the prophet did not list Egypt among Russia's allies in this
invasion. But with the new disagreements between the

Communists of the Kremlin and Israel's perennial enemy of the Nile, perhaps we are seeing why Egypt was not given as an ally. In fact it is easier now to see Egypt as a planned victim of the invasion, though the Russians will not get nearly that far with their plans. The present growing animosity in the United Nations and among the Third World countries in general toward little Israel suggests a justification for Russia to act militarily. In the light of the most current events it is hard to appreciate, but none of this was even a vague possibility on the world scene only ten years ago.

We have seen that the Tribulation period is to start with a peace covenant between the Antichrist and Israel, and it is remarkable that such attempts at peace for Israel are constantly in the offing today. The Sinai peace agreement, engineered by Henry Kissinger in 1975, was a covenant not unlike that which is to begin the Tribulation period, and it rather sets the stage for it. Naturally the Israelis would prefer a seven-year pact to the temporary type of arrangements usually made with their hostile neighbors. As we pointed out, the Russian invasion and the Antichrist's covenant may be a cause-and-effect happening; and the two seem to be in simultaneous preparation today. Again, none of this was true ten years ago.

Considering Matthew 24, *all* of the Lord's end-times pronouncements have now been accomplished, though they may yet appear in even greater degree. In regard to verse 5, "For many shall come in my name, saying, I am Christ; and shall deceive many," today we certainly have our share of false messiahs, gurus, and cults galore, who do deceive a great many people. The "wars and rumours of wars" statements (v. 6) need no analysis; our particular generation has probably seen more separate wars, involving more separate nations, than any generation in history. We also have the "famines, and pestilences, and earthquakes" (v. 7) in disproportionate amounts to previous times. Famine is no longer an isolated tragedy in today's world; the pestilences that accompany famine, and the outbreaks of cholera, not to mention the rise of venereal disease, mysterious epidemics, and even the coming of the "killer bees," seem to establish all too well the pestilence prophecy; our earthquakes indeed happen "in divers places" and with more frequency than in any generation as far back as earthquakes have been recorded.

The Lord went on in Matthew 24 to describe the human condition in the end times, and sadly, our world today qualifies in this area, too. The Lord lamented, "And then shall many be offended, and shall betray one another, and shall hate one another" (v. 10). We have no need to detail the pure unkindness of men toward one another in the world today. The corruption in governments, the cheating in business, the racial hatreds, and all of the inhumanities of the ages seem to have reached a fever pitch today. "And because iniquity shall abound, the love of many shall wax cold" (v. 12). Indeed, we can lament divorce statistics today that no previous generation can compete with. Our pornography, our "free" love, and the entire deterioration of our personal moral values have made the old standard of love grow very cold today.

More subtle phenomena in today's world that appear to be Tribulation-period oriented are the various ramifications of a one-world system in money, the apostate church, and government. Today we have ever increasing international trade, a worldwide movement toward an ecumenical (unbelieving) church, and a World Court, which increasingly interprets principles of a (new) international law. The book of Revelation describes all three of these phenomena as part of the Antichrist's world-dominating system.

It is becoming difficult to separate fact from rumor, for excited Christians try to find prophecy fulfillment in just about everything these days. But, supposedly, gigantic computers are being set up that will be capable of keeping track of the buying and selling of the global public, in the manner that the Antichrist will undertake. One in Belgium is reportedly called (affectionately) "The Beast" by its programmers, who are overwhelmed by its size and capabilities. The Antichrist is referred to as "the beast" throughout Revelation. There is no doubt of the increasing use of numbers to identify citizens, as with the use of social security numbers to keep track of university students or soldiers, and of course this is a hallmark of the Antichrist's procedure. He will give everyone a number, Revelation tells us, which will be "the mark of the beast," and which will be mandatory for buying and selling. We have not seen human beings stamped with any special numbers thus far, although this is reportedly being contemplated by American supermarket chains, but we do see digital number markings on the actual foodstuffs on all supermarket shelves today. Those thin and thick lines on the labels of virtually every item are to be read by scanning machines in the checkout line. It is likely only a short and logical step to asking the customers to have an invisible number imprinted on their persons in order that accurate charges be made. The number would be similar to those made by stamping devices used at amusement parks and other places; the numbers show up under a special light. Those setting up such procedures do not appear to be promoting any sort of evil; they only want to make buying and selling more efficient and secure. But it appears that the devil will make good use of their systems.

One unmistakable sign of the Tribulation period stated in Revelation is the appearance of the fearsome two hundred million-man army to be marched on Israel by the king of the east. This prodigious force, which will take part in the battle at Armageddon, was impossible until this generation. No nation could have fielded such an army. But now the People's Republic of China can do this, and its fits with the Chinese mentality of every man working or fighting for the state. China can march two hundred million able-bodied men to war today, but just ten years ago they could not have. There are probably not enough ships and planes in the whole world to transport such an army, and that is why the eastern king will march his troops, despite the distance. Also, marching soldiers never outrun their supplies; they can find their food and water as they go, rather than having to depend on long-distance support.

The mighty Euphrates River is an appreciable obstacle to any marching force coming to the Middle East, but Revelation sees it dried up in the end times. How shall this come about? Actually, it is drying up already in Iraq. The Russians built a dam in Iran recently, and there is a present squabble over its use in that country. Iraq, located downstream, is not getting the water it used to receive from the Euphrates, and official protests have been raised. Once a dam is in place, the controller of that dam can dry up its river at will. Apparently the king of the east will march his army over a dry riverbed on his way to Armageddon.

A final point concerned with the Revelation picture of the end times has to do with the general direction of the world's spiritual state. It would have been hard to imagine all this evil coming into the world a century ago, for example, because men were simply more oriented to their

Creator then. Before the theory of evolution gained such prominence, scientists assumed that the world had a Creator. Probably a great portion of mankind, and especially the majority of the Western world, had a real appreciation of God's presence, if not a saving faith. The great American and European universities were initially founded as divinity schools, with the Bible being considered as extremely relevant and worthwhile study material.

But now all that has changed. Today atheism has become dominant in the world as socialistic philosophies control enormous numbers of people, and new nations form easily under the godless red flag. It has become an intellectual tradition to reject the Creator and to consider the Bible mythological. Bible criticism is held in higher esteem than Bible belief at universities, and the nature of Christian-principled government is changing. The American government was formed very definitely with regard to God, in whom the founding fathers trusted; but it is now becoming much less concerned with individual rights, honesty, and moral rightness. With the decline of Christianity in the United States and the Western world in general, the stage is philosophically set for a totally atheistic world ruler to enter the picture. He might have been rejected by the world a century ago, but much groundwork has been laid for his appearance now.

It is significant in this regard that so great a portion of even Israel is nonreligious today. It has become the norm in the world to be without God, not with Him, and even the chosen people, who have founded an essentially religious state confined to their own religion as much as possible, have fallen into apostate ways. What a good time for the head atheist to make his dictatorial appearance. What a good time for him to bring a peace covenant. What a good time for the world to throw out the last remains of

what it considers to be a dead God and get on with the
business of running a cold world of numbered personalities
and fierce struggle for global control.

I do not wish to set a date for the rapture, which is impossible to do, as we can see from Scripture. Nor do I wish
to fall into the trap of seeing all everyday events as con-
tributing to a soon Tribulation period. But I do wish to
contrast the present with the past in the hope of showing a
direction that the world seems to be taking. Bible-reading
people are supplied with prophecy for good reason; we are
not to be caught unawares. We see too many examples of
Israel being caught unawares in the Old Testament, losing
two Temples in the process of their apostasy. "Because
you have not heard My Word," God repeats as His rationale for their hard times in His chastisements of His chosen
ones. The Church today should not fail to heed prophecy
insofar as we can apply it intelligently to what we see
around us. We shall make some mistakes, in all probability,
but if we keep the Scriptures foremost in our thinking, we
shall be conscious of God's plan moving onward in the
world.

With that spirit in view, I wish to present the ultimate
argument for a soon Tribulation period, with all its suppo-
sitions as well as its strong points. I refer to Jesus' remarkable statement in Matthew 24:34:

> Verily I say unto you, This generation shall not pass, till
> all these things be fulfilled.

There is certainly a lot of conjecture as to what Jesus
meant by that. Did He mean to tell the disciples that they
themselves would see the Tribulation prophecies worked
out in their lifetimes? If so, that apparently did not happen. Does the term *generation* perhaps refer to a race
(*genera*) of people, and the Lord was only pointing out

that the Jewish nation would not perish until all the prophecies were accomplished? That is certainly possible, but then Jesus would have been saying something that was said many times before by the prophets. Indeed, the nation of Israel, it was written, would outlast the world (Jer 31:37). The Lord did not need to spell out the survival of the chosen people once again. We would expect, instead, in the context of so much detailed prophecy, that He would say something new to answer the disciples' question.

Some analysts hold that there is a special generation of people somewhere in time who will see the Lord's prophecies fulfilled, and that is the generation that will see His return.

This concept of the Lord's statement has led many prophecy analysts into unsure territory. They have tried to fix a given generation, to pick its starting point, as it were. They have created their own clock, which is to put the Lord on a schedule. It needs to be said clearly that this has been tried many times in the past, with many different generations selected for their supposed similarity to the Lord's prescription, with failure every time. We are particularly seeing this kind of reasoning going on in the present generation, with its starting point usually set in 1948, when Israel was regathered to the land. This has led to date-setting for the end times, with many assumptions as to how long a generation lasts, what events exactly fulfill the prophecies, and so forth. I do not wish to join the company of those who chose the Civil War, World War I, World War II, and other events as representing the fulfillments of the Lord's prophecies.

Neither do I wish to join the company of those who failed to heed prophecy altogether. I was in their company all my life, until I was saved, and I like my spiritual situation a lot better now!

So I will put my statement on Jesus' prophecy in this way: *If* the Lord meant literally a *generation* of people, in terms of so many years, in His statement, and *if* the phenomena we are seeing in the world today are actually signs of some impending action by God (which none of us can ever say dogmatically), then it seems clear that our particular times jibe better with the Lord's statement than any we have seen so far. As we have followed His prophecies given in Matthew 24, we have seen that we have fulfillments in some measure or other of every one of them today.

I do wish to bend over backward to avoid being a date-setter where prophecy is concerned, but I do not wish to bend so far that I cannot see my Bible in front of me. If the point has been made that this is a good time to witness and that salvation is available for a limited time only, however long or short that time may be, then I have accomplished my purpose. If in this book about the Jews I have illustrated that the Jewish future holds many tears, or, as the Lord better said it, "gnashing of teeth," then we are all forewarned that this is the hour to fulfill the Lord's command to take the Gospel "to the Jew first." If my own little collection of "prophecy fulfillments" has any validity at all, then it is certainly time to act evangelically.

And all this prophecy brings us to a very subtle additional reason the Jew does not want his Messiah. Look at it this way: if you had some hearsay evidence that impending doom was a possibility for you and your neighbors, you would tend not to want to hear about it. That is just the way people are. There is a psychological defense mechanism called *denial*, through which all of us, in tight spots, ignore the evidence of something very negative coming upon us. The American people and the Russian people hold to détente and shaky agreements about limiting nuclear arms in spite of the many violations of both solutions to our problems that are part of daily news. In simpler examples, we tend not to want to know the ultimate truth of the doctor's diagnosis when we are seriously ill; business men tend not to want to hear from their accountants when their tax bill is going to be a burden; we will ignore the evidence of a toothache until it is overwhelmingly painful, because we do not want to face the dentist; and that ping in the car engine gets little attention. Sometimes it is easier to say, "Don't tell me about it" than to plan for some negative eventuality.

And that may be what a lot of Jews are saying. They have heard about prophecy. They may be distracted from the Scriptures by the rituals of their present form of Judaism, but they realize that the Scriptures prophesy an unhappy ending for the godless world. Many times throughout their history they have been lost in apostasy, but they have never been stupid. These days, when modern Bible translations are freely available in drugstores and department stores, and when Christian radio and television witness daily, and when the true Church is making some real noise in the world about Christ, the Jews have heard a good deal about what their own Book predicts.

But they are presently in an "if I ignore it, it might go away" frame of mind. Maybe the Church will start preaching something more palatable, they hope, and they sort of hold their ears. They reacted the same way to the prophets and to the Messiah; they did not want to know about the visions of Isaiah and Jeremiah regarding the impending Babylonian invasion and resulting captivity; they tried to wipe out all memory of the sincere Galilean who cried, "O Jerusalem!" and told them that yet another Temple was doomed (Matt 23:37-38).

Again, who can blame them? If Christians had ever seen what the Jews have seen in the same way of persecution, hatred, and judgments of God, then they would say, "Don't tell us about it. We just don't want to hear any more."

But of course this attitude must be overcome if the Jew is to avoid the consequences this time. And the consequences *this time* are something to avoid! This time represents the utter end for all Jews who resist God's solution; we know it, and they can be made to know it. This time is not like the wilderness, where the people were disciplined; nor the captivity, which they survived; nor even the dispersion, which they overcame; this time is for "all the marbles." The Jew simply *must* face God's terms this time, or there will be no other chance.

I need say no more about the prophecy situation or how it argues for a redoubled Christian effort to bring God's chosen people, and all other people, to God. We shall not succeed in saving the world, it is written, but we have the privilege, indeed, the duty, of bringing to salvation all we can reach. Those we forgive on earth, the Lord said, are forgiven in heaven. Our God forgave the Jews so many times. Surely we can do so now, and we can overcome all of their objections to the Messiah—psychological, theological, and even those that are a result of blindness (our Lord healed the blind and told us that we would do even "greater works than these," John 14:12).

We must, as we pray, keep in mind that our times may be different than any other times before us. We may have a new situation today, as regards the Jews and everybody else.

The Lord is still invariably available to all, but perhaps today it is "for a limited time only."

9

"How Did You Treat My Brothers?"

I don't want to take up a big chapter talking about my Christian experience or testimony, but I do just want to say that I used to be a Jew who didn't want his Messiah, or anybody's messiah, and now I've changed.

Now I'm a Christian (or a Hebrew Christian, if you must), and my life has utterly turned upside down and backward, all to the good. (Question I once received in a question-answer period in a church: What is the proper term for a Jewish person who has come to Jesus Christ?" Answer: "Christian.")

I have indicated that my Jewish background contained a reasonable, more than average, amount of Jewish training, and a comprehension of the Jewish community from the inside. I was thirty-two years old before I was saved, so I had some experience as an unsaved Jew.

And I wouldn't go through that again for anything. Personally, I think Judaism is the world's best religion, but I'm no longer interested in the world's religions. I belong now to the Kingdom that is "not of this world," and I eagerly await my King.

What's the difference in me since Christ started taking care of my life? Well, first, I love Zola Levitt, an accomplishment that few people, including myself, were tempted to try previously. Seriously, I now can appreciate that I am made in God's image, and I never could imagine what He meant by that before. I'm like God in that my first interest now is love. Believe me, I have love for me, love for you, and love for everybody else, as long as I am following my Lord. I was unable to follow Him before, because I had not met Him.

Second, I feel *really* saved. I know where I'm going when I die, if the Lord tarries that long, and I know where I'm going every day that I live. I really know that my sins are forgiven, and I'm glad of that. I'm glad God is willing to see me in the "robes of righteousness" of Jesus, because I would never make it on my own. I am truly thankful to my Brother of the tribe of Judah for willingly going to the cross for this errant member of the tribe of Levi and for everybody else.

Third, I have useful, gratifying, fascinating work to do in this world while I live, and a Supervisor who makes policies I can live with. If He calls me to write a new book tomorrow morning, I'll be glad. If He calls me to roll out of the sack at dawn to go stand in the rain and witness to some Jewish brother (as He has done so often), I'll be glad. If He calls me home to Him, I'm more than ready to go, and I'll be very glad.

Fourth (and I could go on and on with *these* blessings), I'm "light on my feet"—glad to be alive. I'm very excited. I'm enthusiastic about my life, and I used to be a terrible cynic about things. Increasingly, as I have accurately followed my Lord, I have become energetic about life until I almost can't sit still. I have some sins left over from my earlier times, but so many have left me in the past six years that I never bother about that. The Lord says "Whoa" now and then, and I've learned to listen and profit, as with a good teacher.

The new covenant was a great idea, as far as I'm concerned, and it is surely the only way a sinning, skeptical, spiritual runt like me would ever have gotten home to God. I'm glad it was paid for in advance, because I personally would not have gone to the cross to save my people. I'm glad that the One who paid my debts in full came back to be with me and change my life. I'm glad He came as a man and as a Jew, because I know that made Him just like me; and, therefore, I know that when He returns, I'll be just like Him.

When I made my first hesitant steps toward the Messiah, I said to Him, "If You're there, show me." What a way to talk to God! But He's used to it. Especially from *my* people. He showed me, in wonderful, subtle ways that were and are a secret between Him and me. I don't keep my blessings a secret because there is something wrong with them, but because they have meaning only to me. If I told you that my thinking and my patterns of "being me" changed overnight, I wouldn't be telling you anything useful.

But if I told you that He'll gladly do the same for you— *right now, this minute*—then I'm telling you something very useful. It's so useful that I don't know how you've been getting along without it. (Probably about the same as I was.)

I'm not going to tell you all the details of how I came to Christ; they're rather typical, regardless of the fuss made over them by dear Gentile Christians I know. God heals every man as stunningly as He did the lepers and blind men and beggars in the gospel. Anyway, my details are not your details. I got some learning about that in the Los Angeles airport one day, where the Jews for Jesus movement (God bless their tireless, stubborn hearts) hand out pamphlets endlessly. A marvelous-looking, fully bearded, young Jewish man in army fatigues, looking much like a tough Israeli commando, approached me there as I debarked from a flight and handed me a little yellow pamphlet. The front panel said:

> Everything you didn't want to know about Baruch Goldstein*

Baruch is a Hebrew word that means *blessing*, and he certainly was. I just gave him a hug, and I think he understood that I was already saved. If I had the guts to be practically spat upon by passersby, I would have joined them at their hard ministry. I saw one of their helpers, who was a Gentile, wearing a sweatshirt that identified her as "Gentile for Jesus," and my heart has been very glad ever since.

Now, a certain number of people reading this book are Jews—I know that. I know there are Gentiles out there who give my books to Jews even if they get them thrown back at them. If you're a Jew reading this book, and you've read this far, you must have a Gentile Christian friend who loves you very dearly, and you must perceive that. Possibly you bought this book yourself, but I doubt it. Most Jews who pick up my books in a store throw them down like their fingers have been burned (when actually my books are designed to prevent that!).

Now, Mr. Goldstein, Mr. Cohen, Mr. Levine (and you, too, Mr. Smith, even though your grandfather changed his name), I mean everything I have said in this book, and I mean it in the greatest love for you and the rest of my people. You know very well that you're separated from God and that God is yours for the asking. You know very well that He chose you and that He wants you. You know that if you pick up your Tenach and look up the Scriptures I've talked about, they will be there and they will be true.

---

*and really never cared to ask.

You know that I'm not kidding you, and that they, those *goyim*, haven't kidded me. You know by the way I talk that I'm Jewish and that I'm "not so dumb," as we used to say better in Yiddish. You know that I wouldn't come out at you in public this way if I didn't believe in this.

I'll tell you something you can really appreciate, and you'll know that I'm sincere. It's this: This book won't sell!

That's right, this book is largely a waste of time, and a lot of it. This book took me so long to research and write that I had to change some passages, in the final editing, that practically scared me. Did you read when it said that I was a Christian for six years? Well, I had to change that from "three and one-half" years. That's how long I worked on this book that won't sell.

It won't sell because the *goyim* have all but given up on you (not that one who loves you—he bought you a copy; but there are so many more who are plain afraid of you, or just don't care anymore). The *goyim* have about given up on you because (1) many of them don't know any better; (2) many of them consider you too tough to handle (but I know you better); and (3) you've made yourself a perfectly impossible spiritual person.

You have too many pretenses in your faith, and you know it very well. You know it, and your rabbi knows it, but the two of you don't know where else to go. Well, if you've read this far, you *do* know where to go now.

Chaver, brother, go to Him. He loves you. He died for you. And if He had it to do all over again, He would die for you again. You've never had a friend like that One, *Landsmann;* don't turn your back on Him.

Now, to my Christian brothers and sisters: Please give this book to a Jew. I don't expect you to talk "Yiddish-English" as I have above, but, believe me, Jews don't bite. Mail one to a rabbi; "cause a stink," as we say in Yiddish.

There is truth in this book because a lot of God's Word is in it. God's people need God's Word today. They gave it to you. Give it back to them.

We need Jews in the Church. My heart goes out to every church because of the awful lack of knowledge of the customs and the land and the Law of the chosen people. How painful it is to me to answer for well-read Christians the simple questions on the Old Testament: there was no Jew to make a point clear that the Christian had lived with and meditated on. How awful I feel when I have to *defend* the fact that the Last Supper was Passover indeed, and just as the Jews have always held it. How shocked a church is when I get the question, "When Jews receive Christ, do they go on to observe the Christian holidays?" and I answer truthfully and scripturally, "There *are* no Christian holidays. God gave us all our feasts in Leviticus 23, and He fulfilled them all in Christ." (How perplexed even *you* are to read that enigmatic, but very simple, truth of Scripture. Well, can you give me some New Testament holidays or feasts? Actually, the old ones were as good for the new covenant as the Ten Commandments were. You don't have to *keep* the feasts; but if you had a Jew in your church, you'd at least know what they are, why they were given, and to whom they were given.)

"Save a Gentile, get a Christian; save a Jew, get an evangelist," goes an old Christian saying. Watch what happens in your church when you have committed Jews among you, as God prefers. Watch them put their fabled salesmanship to work for the Lord! You can trust them; they have never hurt anyone despite the punishments they have absorbed.

And pray.

Perhaps I should have had a whole chapter on prayer just to ask for prayer and more prayer on behalf of my people. All the evangelism, all the understanding of the Jewish position, all the Bible study in the world won't do as much as the simple intercession with God that our Lord thought so important. I don't know a whole lot about prayer—just that God hears every prayer and answers every prayer. I know that Jesus always took time for it, even when He had but hours to live.

Now that you know something more about why the chosen people don't want their Messiah, use that knowledge. Study the Scriptures, and be ready for the Jewish objections to their own salvation. Be ready to answer to what lies in your heart, as the Scripture admonishes. And glorify God by granting salvation to the chosen people.

Jesus will ask someday, "How did you treat My brothers?" (see Matt 25:40). Do you treat them kindly but avoid upsetting them about Jesus? Do you avoid them altogether? Do you know a Christian group closed to them? (I know of a very large Christian group that moved its usual meeting away from a certain country club so that Jewish Christians could speak before the group. We were well received. Maybe someday we'll qualify for the club itself.)

Do you include your Jewish acquaintances in the love you have that is Christ's? Can you do better? They need you to do better.

Can you bring just one to the Lord in your lifetime? Do you realize that if each American believer brought one Jew to the Messiah, all the Jews in the world would be saved? That's true. There's few of them and many of us, and they couldn't be more hungry in their hearts.

God bless! Godspeed!

I've just prayed between paragraphs.

Won't you pray now?

A current list of Zola Levitt's books, tapes, albums, etc. is available at no charge from:

ZOLA
P. O. Box 12268
Dallas, Texas 75225